SATANISM

A BEGINNER'S GUIDE TO THE RELIGIOUS WORSHIP OF SATAN AND DEMONS

Volume I: Philosophy

BY

BROTHER NERO

DEVIL'S MARK PUBLISHING

Devil's Mark Publishing

Library of Congress Control Number:

2010936550 ISBN 978-0-9842108-0-0

PROJECT MANAGER: Robert J. Womack

EDITOR: Kasey Koon

CO-EDITED BY: Na'amah and Alexandra

www.RJWomack.com

https://www.facebook.com/rjwomack15/

https://twitter.com/rjwo15

From childhood's hour I have not been
As others were—I have not seen
As others saw—I could not bring
My passions from a common spring.
From the same source I have not taken
My sorrow; I could not awaken
My heart to joy at the same tone;
And all I lov'd, *I* lov'd alone.
Then—in my childhood—in the dawn
Of a most stormy life—was drawn
From ev'ry depth of good and ill
The mystery which binds me still:
From the torrent, or the fountain,
From the red cliff of the mountain,
From the sun that 'round me roll'd
In its autumn tint of gold—
From the lightning in the sky
As it pass'd me flying by—
From the thunder and the storm,
And the cloud that took the form
(When the rest of Heaven was blue)
Of a demon in my view.

Edgar Allan Poe,
Alone

TABLE OF CONTENTS

FOREWORD

I would definitely have to say that the book you now hold in your hands has been a long time coming, and I would know better than most. I first met the author, Brother Nero, over eight years ago. I was new to Satanism at the time, and found myself lucky enough to run into Nero and become a student of his. As the years passed, I eventually found myself working with Nero on many projects, some more successful than others. Ultimately, I have filled the role of his official (and sometimes unofficial) personal assistant many times, still continue to do so now and then, and probably always will.

Nero began his life as a Satanist at the age of twelve, and contrary to what many of his detractors may tell you, his Satanism was not the result of rebellion against a strict Christian upbringing. In fact, his childhood was virtually devoid of any serious, meaningful spirituality, Christian or otherwise. Instead, Nero devoted his life to Satan and His cause as a result of personal spiritual revelation, which happens more often in Satanism than one would think.

The last twenty-five years of Nero's life have more than prepared him to write a volume such as this. After spending time as an initiate of both the O.T.O. (Ordo Templi Orientis) and the Temple of Set, it soon became apparent to Nero that these institutions were not adequate vehicles for his religious convictions, and so, in 1992, he founded his own religious body: H.O.M.E. (Horned Order's Magickal Existence.) Unlike the O.T.O. and the Temple of Set, H.O.M.E. was organized as a Satanist body dedicated to traditional religious worship of the Devil instead of being primarily a magical order.

Over the years, H.O.M.E. saw many highs and lows. I became involved with H.O.M.E. in 2002, and tried my best to help Nero achieve his dreams. However, despite mine and others help, it was not enough to save H.O.M.E. from it's eventual demise in 2004.

Since that time, Nero has kept a low profile, being content to continue his ministry by regularly releasing audio sermons to the public. That is, until now. Nero has finally decided to start preserving his teachings in printed format, which is something that many people, including myself, have urged Nero to do for years. This book is unlike any other book published on the theory and practice of Traditional Satanism. Nero holds no punches, tells no bullshit, and won't pull your leg. He may shock you, he may even disturb you, but he definitely will not bore you or fail to show you the thoughts of a man who has truly devoted his life and soul to the Lord of Darkness.

If you are unacquainted with Nero's way of thinking, I don't want to take away from the impact of his ideas by analyzing them in this forward before you read them in his own words. Many Satanists who read this book may disagree with a few, or a lot, of the things said in here. Hell, I myself don't agree completely with ALL of Nero's views, but one thing is sure: this man is not kidding. He practices everything he preaches (and then some, for that matter.) So, without any further rambling on my part, I am proud to present to you the first book by Brother Nero, a man who was once my High Priest, is now my boss at Devil's Mark Publishing, and who will always be a deeply loved and cherished friend. To quote a famous dead bald guy: "Here is Satanic thought from a truly Satanic point of view."

- BROTHER OBITUS

INTRODUCTION

OVER the years, there have been many books written on the subject of Satanism, but very few of them that have been presented from the perspective of those who actually worship Satan. In my opinion, there has never been a book produced that takes an in-depth look at the religious beliefs and practices of those who worship Satan, or has given an adequate cosmological and theological basis for these beliefs.

More often than not, when books are written or documentaries are produced about Satanism, they rarely mention those of us who believe in the literal existence of Satan and worship him as our god. Not only do these filmmakers and writers not mention us, but many of them act like we don't even exist. In their minds, people who actually worship Satan seem to be just as much a myth or superstition as they believe Satan himself to be. The image of Devil Worshipers, as some people like to call us, is so negative that many people in our society find it almost impossible to believe that anyone would willingly worship Satan. It never occurs to them that maybe their perception of Satan or Satanists is incorrect, or that they may have been misinformed about what we believe and why.

If Satan chooses not to answer someone who calls out to him, or he doesn't feel the need to prove his existence to atheists, scientists, or run-of-the-mill skeptics, it doesn't mean he does not exist. It simply means that for whatever reason, Satan has chosen not to reveal himself to these people. Just like us, Demonic spirits can choose who they want to communicate with.

They are under no obligation to prove themselves or their existence. They do not have to justify who they are to anyone, especially not to people who do not have any respect for them.

The primary goal of this book is to promote the religious worship of Satan as a serious faith and way of life. My secondary goal in writing this book is to preserve the H.O.M.E.* approach to Traditional Satanism. It is my hope this book will provide you with much of the information you will need to get started on your path in Satanism. I also hope it provides you with the information you need to start making Satan and his Demons an important part of your everyday life, because that is what worshiping Satan is all about – building a relationship with Satan and his Demons. Practicing Satanism without developing a relationship with Satan and the other Demonic spirits is like drinking beer without the alcohol. What's the point? You get nothing out of it.

Over the years I have met many Satanists, and I have seen many of them become obsessed with obtaining knowledge, power, or that one occult secret that will make them a great magician. The majority of them overlook the most important occult secret of all, which is building a relationship with Satan and the Demons.

In order to build that relationship you must be able to humble yourself enough to accept that there are forces and beings in this universe more knowledgeable and more powerful than yourself. You must also understand that Satan and the Demons are not fairy godmothers or

---

* Horned Order's Magickal Existence. A Traditional Satanism Church founded by Brother Nero in 1992. He served as High Priest of that organization until it's demise in 2005. – ED.

genies who will fulfill your every wish. They are spiritual entities who all have individual personalities and personal preferences just like we do, and making a connection with them and developing an understanding of them takes time. This relationship goes both ways, and if you help them, they will help you. If you show them respect, more often than not they will do the same in return.

The spiritual bond I am talking about is not something you can get by joining a Satanic group or by reading books on Satanism. It is a connection that is between each individual Satanist and the Demonic spirits. You cannot describe it or even understand it if you have never experienced it for yourself. It is a gift that only Satan can give. That is the true secret of this religion. It is the one thing that distinguishes the real Satanists from the people who like to dress up in black robes and wear pentagrams just because they think Satan is cool.

If you ask any serious Traditional Satanist what it is like, they would tell you without exception that Traditional Satanism is one of the most difficult religions to practice. As a Traditional Satanist, you are truly an outcast in the eyes of most people in our society. Not only are you persecuted by Christians and atheists for what you believe, but you are likely to be criticized by modern Satanists, Wiccans, Thelemites, and countless other religious groups, simply because you worship Satan. The only group the general public hates more than they hate us are white supremacists.

You certainly will not get any argument from me that Traditional Satanism is one of the toughest religions to follow because of the negative impression the public has of our religion. However, I can also say with all sincerity that Traditional Satanism can be one of the most rewarding and uplifting spiritual journeys you can take. That is, if you understand that there truly is a genuine beauty in the things which our society calls evil, and a light in the darkness, and that His name is Satan. Having a relationship with Satan is far more important to me than anything anyone might put me through.

CHAPTER I

SATAN

EVERYBODY always asks "Why do you worship Satan?" And it is usually a person who is totally flabbergasted by the idea that anyone would worship Satan, because they are either a Christian or they are somebody who has bought into the whole Christian attitude about Satan. In this chapter I am going to take some time to explain to you a little bit about the beliefs that our philosophy is based on, the beliefs that I hold to be the truth. And I want you to understand that the things I write about in this chapter are, in my opinion, the objective reality of the universe.

The reason I worship Satan, the reason I teach what I do, and the reason this book is here is because I believe Satan, in his Luciferian form, gave mankind knowledge, wisdom, and self-awareness. He, along with the other Demons (which some people refer to as the Nephilim, or the Watchers), planted the seed for medicine, science, and the modern technologies we have today. By whatever name you want to call them, these Demons gave mankind a true understanding of their own potential. They gave us the ability to think for ourselves.

But most importantly, they gave us self-awareness and freedom, and gave us the ability to understand our universe and the world around us, and to develop our intellect. With that in mind, we worship them as a way of showing respect and appreciation, and remembering the gift of self-awareness that they gave us, because we believe that without Satan and the Demons, mankind would be nothing but mindless slaves to the Judaeo-Christian god.

A lot of people will say, "That's reverse Christianity!" but I don't care what those people think. I don't care if they think we're reverse Christians. I don't care about their opinions, because from what I have experienced, from what I have witnessed with my own two eyes, and from my own ritual practice, I believe this to be the truth, and I am going to preach the truth.

Now I know you might be saying to yourself, "Well, how do I know you're preaching what you really believe, and it's not just a gimmick, or just something you're doing to get attention?" Anybody who knows me will tell you that anything that I say in this book I believe and I live by, and that is the whole reason I wrote this book. The things that I believe may be controversial, but they are not controversial merely for the sake of being controversial. They are what I truly believe.

If I present an opinion in this book that is controversial, it is not merely for the sake of being provocative. It is because I believe there is a valid reason behind the point of view I am presenting, and it has a purpose: either to preserve our religious traditions or assist us in promulgating our religious faith. Nothing in this book has been written merely for shock value. I want people to start living this religion, living these beliefs, and applying these ideas in practice, because I believe that is so much of what the Satanic community is lacking.

Without Satan, mankind is nothing, because the Judaeo-Christian god does not like people to have free will, and does not like people to do anything that he does not approve of. The entire reason mankind was created, according to our particular tradition of Satanism, was to be a slave to Jehovah, and he derives his power to exist through prayer, guilt, and the selfless worship of his followers. In Revelation 4:8[1] we see an example of the Christian god's constant desire for praise and worship. This is a sign of his narcissism, but the spiritual implications go much deeper than that.

We believe that this constant praise and worship is the source of the Christian god's power that allows him to continue to exist. Without this constant worship and praise from his angels, his followers, and other spiritual beings, he would cease to exist, and he would have no influence over the world as we know it. Further verses such as Revelation 4:10[2] give us an indication of what an eternal life in Heaven would be like, catering to his ego and every whim for eternity, and who in their right mind would really want to do that? We believe this is the very reason why Satan and his angels departed the heavenly realm. Why would beings with such a superior level of intelligence want to submit to the slavery of the Christian god?

Satan, on the other hand, not only gets his power from the worship of his followers, but he also gets power from sacrificial offerings, sexual activity, and other natural human emotions. It has been widely accepted for centuries that Satan and the Demons get energy from sexual intercourse that is engaged in during rituals, as well as all the human emotions that go along with it. The energy they get from sacrificial offerings is

---

1 "And the four beasts had each of them six wings about him; and they were full of eyes within: and they rest not day and night, saying, Holy, holy, holy, Lord God Almighty, which was, and is, and is to come."

2 "The four and twenty elders fall down before him that sat on the throne, and worship him that liveth for ever and ever, and cast their crowns before the throne."

derived from the life force of the sacrifice being offered.

The information I am presenting in this book about sacrifice and the way to worship Satan is based on the practical experience of myself and other Satanists that I know, in addition to information provided by those who came before us, such as the medieval witches. We have people who base their whole website, religious belief, philosophy, and group on what they read, and only what they read. Not much of it is based on practical experience, and that is what I would like to see change. The things I bring up are things that I have experienced firsthand, and that I know to be truth because of that experience. Whether you believe me or not is entirely up to you, and everybody is entitled to their own opinions, but to me, this is not a game. This is not a joke. This is not something I do to entertain myself.

I am a Satanist when I get up in the morning. I am a Satanist when I go to bed at night. My opinions and my beliefs are not based on whether they are popular or whether people read this book. Whether ten people that read it or a thousand people read it, it does not matter. The message will always be the same. Why? Because I have a higher power that I answer to, and that is Satan, and his views do not change based on people's opinions, or what's popular on the internet, or who's got the best website this week. They stay the same.

Just because somebody is good at promoting a philosophy they call Satanism does not mean that it actually is. Somebody has to be out here telling the truth, and telling it like it is, and if you study and do the rituals, you will find that's exactly what I am doing. The true secret of Satanism, if you will, is that no matter how many rituals you do, no matter how expensive your robe is, and no matter what organizations you join, it doesn't amount to anything without building a relationship with Satan and his Demons. This relationship is not something you can buy or that an occult organization can sell you. It is either something that you have cultivated, or you haven't.

If the Demons do not want to communicate with you, they won't. If they do, they will. And if they want to reveal the truth of what I am saying, they can. It's not in my power to prove to you that what I am telling you is true. The only thing I can do is preach the message, and hope that Satan guides the right people to this book, and hope that by writing this book I have given you information that will help you. If I have done something to help one person change their attitude, and their approach, and the way they think, and respect Satan and the Demons more than they did in the past, then I have done my job.

SATAN'S GIFT TO MANKIND

As a result of this knowledge that Satan gave to mankind, man was able think for himself and he began to understand, because of his new self-awareness, that there were other ways to look at things besides the Christian god's way. Of course this made Jehovah angry, so he put the curse of mortal death on mankind[3], caused women to have pain during childbirth, and declared war on Satan, as we can clearly see in chapter three of Genesis.[4] As a result of Satan's action, it is clear that the

3 Genesis 3:22-23: And the LORD God said, Behold, the man is become as one of us, to know good and evil: and now, lest he put forth his hand, and take also of the tree of life, and eat, and live for ever. Therefore the LORD God sent him forth from the garden of Eden, to till the ground from whence he was taken.

4 Genesis 3:14-19: And the LORD God said unto the serpent, Because thou

earth was altered in some way and the spirit of man was forever changed, because the scales of ignorance had fallen from his eyes.

Some Satanists have suggested that this event, along with other things, is why God's power is not as evident in the world today and why he seems to take very little interest in the affairs of mankind. When Satan altered mankind's soul and everything on earth, by that very action he became the Lord of this World.[5] Once the world had been altered by Satan, Jehovah hated the earth and its inhabitants, for it was no longer truly his. Because of the free will that Satan gave us, mankind was free to do whatever he wanted, including those things which Jehovah considered evil, and it made him regret making us, because we were no longer solely his creation – we were also Satan's.[6]

---

hast done this, thou art cursed above all cattle, and above every beast of the field; upon thy belly shalt thou go, and dust shalt thou eat all the days of thy life: And I will put enmity between thee and the woman, and between thy seed and her seed; it shall bruise thy head, and thou shalt bruise his heel. Unto the woman he said, I will greatly multiply thy sorrow and thy conception; in sorrow thou shalt bring forth children; and thy desire shall be to thy husband, and he shall rule over thee. And unto Adam he said, Because thou hast hearkened unto the voice of thy wife, and hast eaten of the tree, of which I commanded thee, saying, Thou shalt not eat of it: cursed is the ground for thy sake; in sorrow shalt thou eat of it all the days of thy life; Thorns also and thistles shall it bring forth to thee; and thou shalt eat the herb of the field; In the sweat of thy face shalt thou eat bread, till thou return unto the ground; for out of it wast thou taken: for dust thou art, and unto dust shalt thou return.

5 Ephesians 2:2: Wherein in time past ye walked according to the course of this world, according to the prince of the power of the air [Satan], the spirit that now worketh in the children of disobedience.

6 Genesis 6:5-6: And GOD saw that the wickedness of man was great in the earth, and that every imagination of the thoughts of his heart was only evil continually. And it repented the LORD that he had made man on the earth, and it grieved him at his heart.

Many Christian denominations like to promote the idea that Satan is evil, and his only motivation for interacting with man is ultimately to destroy him. While it is naive to assume that Satan's sole motivation for helping us was to free us from the Judaeo-Christian god's tyranny, we do not believe that the purpose of his intervention was to lead man to his destruction. In my beliefs, Satan's purpose is first and foremost to preserve himself, then his Demons, and lastly us. Aside from the fact that it is very possible that Satan and his Demons interacted on our behalf because they sympathized with our plight, it is clear that another motivation was to have those among mankind who felt a connection with Satan help him in his war against the Judaeo-Christian god.

It is clear that Jehovah fears one thing above all else: the unification of man[7], because this unification of mankind towards the sole objective of destroying Jehovah and his kingdom will almost ensure victory for Satan, especially if the unification is orchestrated and eventually led by Satan. That is why Satan says in the *Al-Jilwah*, "It is my desire that all my followers shall unite in a bond of unity, lest those who are without prevail against them."[8] Satan's desire to involve mankind in his war against god and his angels is not evil; it is just good strategy. Any good general will use whatever means necessary to ensure the survival of himself and his soldiers.

The strength that Satan has that the Judaeo-Christian

7 Genesis 11:6 And the LORD said, Behold, the people is one, and they have all one language; and this they begin to do: and now nothing will be restrained from them, which they have imagined to do.

8 "those who are without" refers to anyone who is not a Satanist.

god does not is that he is not constrained by moral concepts such as good and evil. He can adjust his morality to fit any situation, thereby ensuring that he can make the most appropriate decision for the circumstances that may arise, and securing his and his followers' survival.[9] His main priority is his own self-preservation, and if you want to continue to exist and maintain your own power, then you will do whatever is necessary to hold on to that power.

It should be noted that members of a true Coven should base their moral code on Satan's example. Just like Satan, Traditional Satanists do not have morals *as such*. We have "boundaries." Morals are things that are fixed and unchangeable, like the Ten Commandments. Boundaries are principles that we have that can be adjusted based on the circumstances and situations that arise. For example, you may decide with your partner to maintain a monogamous relationship, but later you find out that your partner is unable to conceive a child. A Satanic couple would simply adapt to the situation and bring another Satanist into the relationship for the purpose of bearing a child, and then raise that child as their own.

Most Satanic couples do not have the moral hang-ups those who are without would have; also, in Traditional Satanism there is no prohibition against having multiple sex partners in a relationship. Unlike many Christian couples who might choose to go the medical route and use artificial insemination, a Satanic couple is more likely to bring another Satanist in and impregnate them the old-fashioned way. By doing this, they not only live by the morals they claim to believe in, but it also saves

9 I participate in all the affairs which those who are without call evil because their nature is not such as they approve. (Al-Jilwah)

them the expense and hassle of having to undergo a medical procedure.

Many people ask, "Is Satan evil?" If you define Satan by a Christian moral code, then the answer is yes, absolutely. But if you define him by a Satanic moral code, we would say that he is not evil. He is just a realist who understands what truly motivates man and makes him strive for greatness. But if we allow Satan to define himself, he says it best: "I participate in all the affairs which those who are without call evil because their nature is not such as they approve."

THE RELATIONSHIP BETWEEN SATAN AND HIS DEMONS

Many people have the misconception that the Demons who serve Satan serve him out of fear or because they are his slaves, but nothing could be further from the truth. The relationship between Satan and his Demons is much like the bond between siblings. They seem to have a genuine love and appreciation for one another, and are motivated by the same goals, chief among these being the destruction of the Christian god and his followers.

In Traditional Satanism, Demons are held in very high regard, and seen as gods in their own right, and we believe that being disrespectful to any Demon would be the same as being disrespectful to Satan himself. That is why one of the aims of my ministry is to bring back the holidays and traditions that were once observed for the chief spirits in Satan's kingdom.[10] The hierarchical structure of Hell has not been put in place to denote

10 For example, Astaroth, Lilith, Belial, Abaddon, etc.

inferiority amongst the spirits, but out of necessity. Just as kingdoms on earth must have order and their rulers must impose a structure, Satan's kingdom is no exception.

CHAPTER II

SATAN AND DEMONS

AN OBJECTIVE REALITY OF THE UNIVERSE

WHEN you first tell someone that you worship Satan, their reaction is usually one of disbelief. People think you are joking or that you are doing it just to get attention. Most people, because of their Christian upbringing, cannot even grasp that there may be people with a different opinion about Satan and his motives. It never occurs to these individuals that there are some of us who honestly believe the Bible and its transcribers are purposely dishonest about the facts surrounding the creation of the world and Satan.

In addition to the people that cannot get beyond the Christian beliefs about Satan, there are those who absolutely refuse to even entertain the idea that Satan might actually exist because of their own negative religious experiences or lack of spiritual encounters. Consequently, these individuals feel compelled not only to ignore any evidence that is presented to them of Satan's existence, but they also feel that they must do everything in their power to belittle those who actually do believe in him and worship him. People who openly believe in the literal existence of Satan and worship him are often characterized as backwards, ignorant, non-thinking people. But the simple truth is, it is not the people who believe in the spirit world or in the literal existence of Satan who are ignorant, it is the individuals who believe in only what can be seen in the physical world.

People have become so enamored with technology

and engrossed in material things that they have become spiritually disconnected. As I heard one author put it recently during a radio interview, the more technologically advanced mankind becomes, the less spiritually aware we are. I totally agree with this opinion: people who do not believe spiritual entities exist will say to someone like me that there is no evidence that God, Satan, the angels, or the Demons exist. But what very few people understand is that in order for you to have strong spiritual experiences, or at least make it easier for them to occur, you should come to these experiences with an open mind and a willingness to experience anything that may happen. That is not to say that the individual has to believe in the spirits in order for them to make themselves known, it just makes it a lot easier if there is not a psychological or emotional barrier hindering their attempts at communication.

As we become more technologically advanced, we are truly going through a spiritual devolution. We seem to have lost touch with the old ways and the origins of our creation. That is one of the main reasons I focus on the religious aspects of Satanism and the worship of Satan more than any other area of our religion. I believe it is this spiritual awareness that Satanists are in such desperate need of if they hope to have any relationship with Satan or to have any understanding of his kingdom. Most Satanists who have any first-hand experience with Demonic spirits understand something that many non-spiritual people do not. If you close yourself off to the Demonic spirits and ignore them, either because you do not believe, or because you are not willing to take the time out of your busy schedule to meditate upon these forces, they will ignore you.

The minute you acknowledge them, these forces will start to reveal themselves to you and will start to interact in your daily life. You will begin to notice changes and you will become more spiritually aware of things happening around you. It is like being born into a reality that you did not know existed, like a veil has been lifted, or scales have been removed from your eyes. As time goes on, you will begin to notice that there are people who see and understand the spirit world in ways that the average person does not, and they are aware of the subtle interactions of the spirits in day-to-day events the same way that you are.

There are some people who refuse to acknowledge the reality of the spirit world regardless of how much evidence is presented to them. In my view, Satan and his Demons are an objective reality of the universe. Almost every culture, regardless of geographical location or religion, has its equivalent of Satan and Demons, and the accounts go back as far as recorded history. The sheer weight of anecdotal evidence alone seems to make the argument that Satan and his Demons are just a myth, or merely the creation of people with overactive imaginations, absolutely laughable. But there are people who still refuse to acknowledge the existence of Satan and his Demons simply because it threatens the elaborate fantasy that they have created for themselves.

It is a well-known fact among many Traditional Satanists that the Demons tend to only show themselves to people who are open-minded enough to show them respect. If you are an individual who has contempt for them, either because you do not believe in them or because you think you already know everything, more often than not, they will not reveal themselves to you.

They are spiritual entities who have emotions and

aspirations just like we do. However, because of their superior intellect and because they have been around since the beginning of time, they have learned how to master themselves in such a way that they have far more control over their emotions than we do. It also seems safe to assume that because they are part of the initial spark that gave rise to all that we can comprehend, they would have a greater understanding of the universe and how it functions. Therefore, they are able to manipulate various universal laws to do things that we would consider supernatural.

It would also not be unreasonable to conclude that because they have been around since the beginning of time, at least as we understand it, that they have played an active role in the evolution of mankind. As a result, their understanding of the human race and what motivates us is much greater than ours. With all this in mind, is it surprising that they may not only have the ability, but also have a genuine desire to see us succeed and grow?

If you look past the superstition and the Christian bias that surrounds medieval manuscripts such as the Goetia, all the evidence suggests that they are not only able to, but have been giving us guidance and instruction about how to understand ourselves so that we can evolve as a species. It should be noted that we are not talking so much about a corporeal evolution, but rather a spiritual one, but many would argue that Satan and the Demons have had a hand in both.

CHAPTER III

SATANIC UNITY AND THE ANTICHRIST

IN this chapter we will be discussing Satanic unity and the Antichrist. The term Antichrist is used in this chapter because it is a term people will be familiar with, and it is the easiest way that I can think of to describe a Satanic spiritual leader, and have everyone invoke the same mental image. But let me be clear: I am not necessarily talking about the Christian concept of the Antichrist. While the leader that I discuss in this chapter may have some similar characteristics to the Antichrist of the Christians, that does not mean that I believe this leader has the same motivations or the same desires to destroy mankind as described in the Christian Bible.

Many individuals in the Satanic community seem to be obsessed with the idea of Satanic unification. They seem to believe that they can do it themselves, without Satan's help. I do not believe we can do it ourselves, that we can unite as a Satanic community. There will always be people who think they are the biggest, baddest motherfuckers around, because that's how Satanists are. All Satanists are egotistical. All Satanists want to be on top. That is a sign of a real Satanist that has the spirit of Satan within them. They want to achieve things; they want to be recognized; they want to be somebody.

Satan is the one who instilled that sense of pride in them, or at least recognized it without judging, if they were a proud person before they became a Satanist. So it would be inappropriate for me to judge them for having ego. There is no shame in having pride in oneself, but there is a difference between having pride in oneself and being an arrogant twat. Having pride in oneself is a consequence of the achievements one has made in life. Arrogance, on the other hand, is having pride in oneself based on no substance and no accomplishments. It is unjustified and unearned.

Unfortunately, far too many people in the Satanic community are arrogant without good reason. They think they know more than they do, and they give themselves titles they have neither earned nor deserve, either through experience or through overcoming one's personal Demons to grow and strengthen themselves as Satanists.

Therein lies the heart of the problem: everyone thinks they are entitled to be a leader, but no one wants to be just a follower. Leaders are only as good as their followers. If you have nobody following you, then you are no leader. If nobody wants to be a follower, then there is no pillar upon which to base the community. And if there is no pillar, then there is no community, and the title you give yourself of Grandmaster of the Universe means absolutely nothing.

As a consequence, the Satanic community is like a large pack of wolves without an alpha male to guide them and show them the way. As everyone knows, a pack without an alpha male and alpha female will slowly devolve into a state of chaos, and members of the pack will turn on each other if it does not have a strong leader to lead it. That is clearly what has been happening and is still happening within the Satanic community. Interestingly enough, Satan/Lucifer is both male and female, as symbolized by the use of Baphomet, which is used to represent both the male and female, active and passive aspects of Satan's nature.

It is important to note that to say Baphomet only represents male and female, or only represents the active and passive nature, would be an oversimplification. What Baphomet truly is is a symbol of all the aspects of Satan in one image, which is considerably more complex and indefinable than just merely saying that it is a symbol of the duality of Satan. He is androgynous, and as a consequence, he can fill both roles within himself, which makes him a perfect alpha leader, and until Satan makes himself known, I believe the Satanic community will continue to devour itself.

The *Al-Jilwah* says it is Satan's desire for us to unite in a bond of unity. Most people fail to realize that it says it is his desire. He did not say it would happen, and I do not believe it will happen without his direct intervention. It is fruitless for us to try to mend all our differences in an attempt to unify, because there will always be somebody who thinks they are better than everyone else and tries to create conflict where there does not need to be any.

The only way the Satanic community can truly put their differences behind them and unite is with supernatural intervention, meaning that Satan himself has to put a hand on the community and guide them to unite. He will take charge of all the followers who swear allegiance to him, and he will do that once he unveils himself and leaves no doubt of his literal existence.

In my personal view, he is likely to make the world aware of his literal existence by manifesting in one of three ways: corporeal, spiritual, or by possessing a human being with his spirit, which would be the Antichrist or Satanic leader that I am talking about. One of these three things has to happen, in my opinion, before the Satanic community can unite, but since Satan prides himself on being unpredictable, he may decide to do something completely different from the above things I mentioned.

Although I believe it is highly likely that one of these three things I mentioned will happen, there is always that element of unpredictability when dealing with Satan or Demons. No matter what form he chooses to manifest himself in, it will be obvious that it is Satan, and it will be obvious to his followers and non-followers alike. He will not need a website. He will not need to convince people to follow him. Just the mere fact that he manifests in any of these forms will be such a cosmic event that everyone in the world will feel it, and they will not have to ask whether it is Satan or his messenger. They will know.

We focus on living our daily lives and working for Satan's cause without concerning ourselves with the End Times, because unlike the followers of the Abrahamic religious traditions, we do not spend our time obsessing over the coming of the Antichrist, Armageddon, or the end of the world. We believe it will be so obvious to everyone that it is Satan manifest that when they see and hear him, they will not have to be told.

All the false titles, and all the false organizations, and all the unnecessary egotism that permeates the Satanic community will evaporate immediately, because those who truly follow Satan will recognize that the true Master has come, and they will either kneel or they will be eliminated. Once Satan has put his house in order, all those who swear allegiance to him will help in the process of eliminating all those who oppose his will. And once Satan eliminates the trash, the eternal, unopposed reign of his kingdom will begin.

CHAPTER IV

PACTS WITH SATAN AND DEMONS

NO guide to practicing Traditional Satanism would be complete without a discussion of pacts with Satan and Demons. When you make a pact with Satan, make sure you write your pact out first, and think about what you are going to say and what you are committing yourself to, because whatever you write, Satan will most likely hold you to the letter of your pact. So don't make grandiose promises you do not intend to keep. If you were smart, you might want to write your entire pact out first, let it sit for the night, and look at it again the following day to be sure that you have worded everything exactly like you meant to.

There is nothing worse than making promises to Satan and then falling short of them, or making promises that you later regret. For example, I had a friend who swore to Satan that he would never date another woman because women got in the way of his relationship with Satan. So, he has made a permanent pact with Satan that he will never date another woman in his life, and he did it primarily because he was upset about a prior relationship.

A pact like this is obviously not the greatest idea in the world, because you are almost guaranteed to fail at keeping the commitment you have made at some point in your life. Nor is a time of high emotional stress where you are likely to say things you later regret a good time to make a pact with Satan. Let me stress again: This story is en example of what you DO NOT want to do.

If you are going to make a pact with Satan or any Demon, you should do it only after you have taken the time to think over the seriousness of the commitments you are making and the possible consequences that may arise as a result of these commitments.

Now let us talk about the different types of pacts an individual can make. The first one is dedicating your soul to Satan's service, which is an eternal pact that is binding not only in this life, but in the afterlife and the lives that are to come. As the *Al-Jilwah* says, "None shall live in this world longer than the time set by me; and if I so desire, I send a person a second or a third time into this world or into some other by the transmigration of souls."

The first thing you should know about a pact like this is that Satan can alter the conditions of the pact at his will, and he can break the pact with you, but you, even if you break your word, cannot sever the pact with him. Even if you fail to fulfill the conditions of the agreement that you have made, it does not invalidate the contract for your soul. He might agree to help you in return for that gift, provided you meet his conditions, but if you break these conditions or the agreement that you have made, it does not necessarily mean that your soul is not still a gift to him. He still owns your soul, regardless of what you do.

Satan or the Demons may allow you to renegotiate the agreements that you have made, but whether you are allowed to do this is entirely at their discretion, not yours. This type of pact is not a temporary pact. It is an eternal pact, and has no expiration date. Many medieval Grimoires cite cases where the Devil has made a pact with somebody for a set period of time – say ten years –

and during that time, he gives them everything their heart desires. At the end of that time period, they die, and their soul belongs to him. An example of a time-dependent pact can be found in Richard Cavendish's book, *The Black Arts*, published in 1967.[11] According to the author, this certain pact was to last for a period of twenty years.

While this may be great fodder for movies and plays, at least in my personal experience and the experiences of many other Satanists I know, Satan doesn't work like that. Once you make a pact with him, he wants you to do as much work for him while you are alive as possible. When you make an eternal pact, you are making an commitment to be a servant and messenger for him. You are not doing it for the purpose of achieving material wealth or fame, or at least you shouldn't be. Now I am not suggesting to you that Satan couldn't or doesn't make those kinds of deals, but I personally have never witnessed a pact like that.

The reason I bring this up is because there are people in the Satanic community who are teaching that you can make a temporary pact with Satan, almost as if having a relationship with Satan is like test-driving a car. If you don't like the way it drives, you can take the car back. But let me assure you: the Lord of Darkness is no fucking car, and if you try to fuck with Satan, and try to outsmart him, you'll end up on the losing end of that

11 My lord and master Lucifer, I acknowledge you as my god and prince, and promise to serve and obey you while I live. And I renounce the other God and Jesus Christ, the saints, the church of Rome and all its sacraments, and all prayers that the faithful may offer me; and I promise to do as much evil as I can and to draw all others to evil; and I renounce chrism, baptism, and all the merits of Jesus Christ and his saints; and if I fail to serve and adore you, paying you homage three times a day, I give you my life as your own. Made this year and day. Signed, Urbain Grandier. (351)

deal every time.

You can make a temporary pact with Satan or Demons, but it's not usually a deal for your soul or committing to their eternal service. It is usually a temporary pact dealing with something more mundane. For example, you can make a pact to do something for a Demon in return for their guidance or their insight, and that pact may have a time limit, but a pact for your soul does not.

If you are going to make a pact with Satan, the best time to do that is on Halloween, because we consider that to be the most sacred holiday to Satan and the day when he is at his most powerful. If for whatever reason you cannot make a pact with Satan on Halloween, make sure you do it during the darkest months of the year. For example, any time between Halloween and Spring Equinox is preferable. The closer it is to Halloween when you make your pact, the better. Nothing in Satan's kingdom comes without a price. You should not get into the habit of making requests of Satan and the Demons without giving some type of offering in return. In the case of pacts with Satan and Demons, it is traditional to give some of your own blood.

When you have completed your pact, you do not literally have to sign your name in blood. You can sign your name with a pen or a quill and then put a spot of blood or drops from the wound that you have made next to the name. This is the way a pact is usually made. I have heard some people suggest that the only way to truly make a pact with Satan is to write the entire pact with blood, as well as the name. This is not only unnecessary but impractical, and is usually an indication that they are probably not practicing Satanists, because the amount of blood needed to write the average pact would be excessive, unless it was short. That does not mean it is impossible, it would just take you a great deal of time. I doubt most of the people who claim to have done their pact this way have actually done it.

CHAPTER V

THE AFTERLIFE

BECAUSE mankind in general fears death, all religions, regardless of tradition, must answer one basic question: what will happen to us when we die? Satanism is no exception. Because so many of us have been raised as part of a Judeo-Christian tradition, we fear what will happen to us in the life hereafter.

Some Satanists, such as the LaVeyans, have decided to answer this question by saying that there is nothing beyond this life. There is no spirit world awaiting us, and therefore, believing in any spiritual entity is a "spiritual pipe-dream."

In Traditional Satanism, we choose not to take such a simplistic view. We believe only idiots think there is no life after death. The sheer weight of anecdotal evidence seems to suggest that there is a spirit world awaiting us when we die.

HELL

Hell is a kingdom created by Satan and ruled by him, where Satanists go to be with him and go to be rewarded for their service to him when they die. It is totally separate and distinct from the Christian god's Lake of Fire or bottomless pit. The bottomless pit or the Lake of Fire referred to in the Bible is the place where Jehovah seeks to put those who refuse to kneel to him if he happens to win the final battle.[12]

12 Revelation 20:10: And the devil that deceived them was cast into the lake of fire and brimstone, where the beast and the false prophet are, and shall be tormented day and night for ever and ever.

There is evidence to suggest that there are many domains within Satan's kingdom, but because we feel it would be imprudent to discuss the structure of Satan's kingdom and the nature of these domains, we will not be discussing them here.

THE POST-MORTEM FATE OF NON-SATANISTS

We believe that when Satanists die they will reside with Satan in his kingdom, and those who are loyal to the Christian god will be with him in his kingdom, and they will stay there until the final battle. Individuals of different religions will be placed in a state of purgatory until a time just before the final battle, at which time they will be allowed to make a choice as to which side they will fight for.

REWARDS AND PUNISHMENTS

Aside from the most obvious questions, which are "Do you believe in the literal existence of Hell?" and "Is it a lake of fire?", the next question is "Will Satan reward his loyal servants, and punish those who are disobedient?"

The *Al-Jilwah*, the Mashaf Resh, and the *Book of the Law* address these questions. "I requite the descendents of Adam, and reward them with various rewards that I alone know." (*Al-Jilwah* ch. II) "All treasures and hidden things are known to me; and as I desire, I take them from one and bestow them upon another." (*Al-*Jilwah *ch. III) "Who dies in my love, I will cast him / In* the midst of Paradise, by my will and pleasure; / But he that dies unmindful of me / Will be thrown into torture in misery and affliction." (The Poem in Praise of Sheikh

Adi, lines 64-67)

"He that dies unmindful of me" is more than likely referring to those who refuse to acknowledge his literal existence and give him the respect he deserves, and he makes it clear that what awaits them will not be pleasant. Chapter II in the *Book of the Law* is associated with Hadit, which Crowley associates with Satan. "Begone! ye mockers; even though ye laugh in my honour ye shall laugh not long: then when ye are sad know that I have forsaken you."

The *Mashaf Resh* takes the same line towards those who deny Satan's existence. "O mine enemies, why do you deny me? O men, deny me not, but submit." ("The Poem in Praise of Sheikh Adi," lines 61-62) Up to this point, Satan has been merciful with those who have been disrespectful and mock his very existence, but I don't believe it will always be that way.

REINCARNATION

In our particular tradition of Satanism we do believe in reincarnation to a certain degree, except that we do not believe the privilege of reincarnation is granted to everyone who is a Satanist. We believe that Satan selects according to his own will who he will send back and for what purpose.[13]

We believe that people who were specifically created to spread his message will come back time and time again in different incarnations to keep spreading his word throughout the centuries, but who that is and when they will come back and in what form they will come

13 None shall live in this world longer than the time set by me; and if I so desire, I send a person a second or a third time into this world or into some other by the transmigration of souls.

back is up to Satan and at his sole discretion.

Over the years I have met many people who have very distinct memories of being in Satan's kingdom, and who believe they have been reincarnated to serve Satan and to preach his philosophy, and almost always, they are Traditional Satanists (or Devil Worshipers). Their accounts are very similar. Usually they were given the choice whether or not to come back. They also often remember being on earth more than once, and some of them are also able to recount their past lives in great detail, even including their name in their last incarnation.

Because of the stories I have heard, I believe in reincarnation much more than I used to. I believe that the individuals who are Traditional Satanists or Devil Worshipers are traditionalists because their soul is ancient and retains an inherent knowledge that makes them aware that Satan and his kingdom exist at an early age.

Also, it may explain why Satanists who come to Satanism at a young age are traditionalists more often than they are modernists, because something gives them a sense of who they are and what their mission is earlier than most ordinary children. Many people are made aware of Satan's presence from the age of twelve into the mid-teens, but there are exceptions to this rule. The earliest age I have heard a child acknowledging Satan's existence and answering his call is at age seven.

Only a fool would continue to believe that there is nothing supernatural going on when a child, at age seven, acknowledges the literal existence of Satan and begins to worship him. I am sure that there are probably some, if they are reading this, who would say that the only reason the child began to worship Satan is because their parents worship Satan. But in the case of the individual I have in mind, she did not grow up in a house full of Satanists, and she had no adults around her practicing Satanism, so that cannot be the reason. So what does this suggest then? It suggests that there is a spiritual reality that few of us can see or understand, and there is a battle for the souls of mankind that will have its inevitable climax in the final battle between the Christian god and Satan.

CHAPTER VI

AM I A SATANIST?

ONE of the most common questions any priest or priestess of Satan is asked is, "How do I know if I'm a Satanist?" or "How do I know that Satan accepts me?" Most people tend to believe they are Satanists if they have a passing interest in "darkness" or horror movies, or because they like to dress like a vampire. Many people find Satan and his darkness intriguing, but this does not necessarily mean they are chosen to be a servant of the Lord of Darkness. In order to be a Satanist, you have to be embraced by – and swear allegiance to – these forces.

You are drawn to it, you reach out to it, and it responds. That is how a relationship is formed between the Satanist and Demonic spirits. First you are drawn to it, which happens to a lot of people, but most of the time that is where their interest stops. The reason is because while Satan and his darkness may fascinate them, they are not brave enough to embrace his ways.

Sometimes they get into other forms of occultism which some people consider "dark", such as vampirism, but this is nothing more than a bunch of people who don't have the balls to look into the eyes of Satan and call him god while pretending to be his children. That is not to say that everyone who is interested in vampirism is a fake, but as with every other area of life, there are people who are the real thing, and then there are the pretenders.

Once you get beyond the individuals who are

pretending to be vampires, Satanists, or witches, there are people who are serious, who are willing to take the next step and perform a ritual or pray to Satan. Among those who are serious, there are two distinct groups: those who are accepted, and those who, for whatever reason, are not.

Though it is impossible for a mortal to know the mind of Satan or Demons, we can at least speculate on some of the possible reasons for why certain individuals are not accepted. Their desire to serve Satan may not be motivated by a genuine love and respect for him, or it may be Satan does not think they are mature enough to understand the seriousness of the commitments they are trying to make. Or it could be something spiritual, which has nothing to do with either one of the things mentioned above, that only Satan himself knows.

A lot of people mistakenly believe that being a Satanist is just a matter of choice. In order to be a Traditional Satanist and have a genuine relationship with Satan or his Demons, you have to get a response. You can't just reach out to them; they have to reach out to you in return. In some cases, Satan or the Demons may actually reach out to an individual first, in which case the individual has only to acknowledge and accept Satan's call. In the case when the Demons reach out to a person first, it is likely (but not an absolute certainty) that this person has served Satan in a previous life, and has been reborn into this world. This may be because they have a specific mission or set of tasks that they must accomplish. The important thing is that both sides reach out to each other and a relationship is forged.

The reason you do not hear more Satanists talk about the importance of a relationship between Satan and his followers is because the majority of Satanists are modernists who do not believe in Satan or Demons. They do not believe in any spirits, because they are atheists. That is one of the key differences between a Traditional Satanist and a modern Satanist. The Traditional Satanist knows that not only is Satan real, but that his Demons are also real. To be a Satanist – to walk down this spiritual path – to truly understand Satan – you must develop a mutual relationship with the spirits.

It should be stressed that Demons do not answer people on the individual's time frame. They do not answer you just because you are getting impatient. They will communicate with you when they want to and how they want to, and some may people try for years before they get any response or indication that Satan accepts them. The Demons' actions do not revolve around us and what we want. They do things that are beneficial to Satan's kingdom according to his time line and not ours. As the *Al-Jilwah* says, "I remember necessary affairs and execute them in due time." Some people may think they have been rejected without realizing that Satan has given them subtle messages all along.

Some people expect Satan or the Demons to express themselves in some over-the-top Hollywood way, and that is not how the Demons usually interact with people. That is not to say that they cannot do these things if or when they so desire, it is just that they very rarely choose to expend that much energy when they can reach a person through other means such as dreams, mental images, and other day-to-day circumstances. That is why, in the chapter talking about magickal journals, we say students should keep a meticulous record of their magickal practices as well as any events that may have spiritual significance, so that they will not miss any subtle communication.

Satan has always said that his children would be few in number. That means that the majority of people that have a fascination with him are not meant to be his children. They just have a fascination with Satan and the dark side of life. Of course, who could blame them for having a fascination with the Lord of Darkness? He's the coolest being in existence, the coolest that has ever existed, and it is natural for mankind to want to be close to an entity that represents raw power, animal magnetism, and has no master because of his pure unholy might.

CHAPTER VII

THE IMPORTANCE OF STANDING UP FOR YOURSELF AND SATAN

WHEN people get into Satanism, especially if they have been in it for a while, they have a tendency to lose focus on the fact that they are Satanists. What I mean by that is, they get so caught up in their daily lives, whether they are a wife, a mother, a father, a businessman, or whatever their particular occupation is – that they forget that they are Satanists. Part of the problem in our religion is that we often put Satanism as a last priority in our lives.

For too many Satanists, Satanism is something they do after everything else. Whatever they do – whatever their responsibilities are – come before being a Satanist, and that is what makes our religion weak. The way we should be thinking is, "I'm a Satanist who also happens to be a mother", "I'm a Satanist who also happens to have a demanding career". The job and the things that you have to do in life should not be your identity or be more important than your god.

If you are truly dedicated to the Satanic religion, it should be a way of life for you. Because that is what it is, after all: a way of life. That is something else a lot of people seem to forget. Satanism is not just a philosophy; it should be a way of living. It should not be an afterthought; it should not be something you add. It should be something you live every day: something that is a part of you, something that is a part of your soul.

Many Satanic groups base their philosophy on

atheism and are more concerned with material wealth than they are with spiritualism. And that is what makes a real Satanist: you cannot take away the spiritual element, because once you do that, it is no longer Satanism. It may have the look of Satanism, it may use terminology that Satanists use, but it is not Satanism.

Satanism should define you as a person. It should be part of what defines your approach to things in life. If you are practicing Satanism seriously and as a way of life, you should use what you learn in Satanism and how Satanism teaches us to approach life in every situation. It should not be something that you do only when other people are not looking. For many Satanists, it is something they hide.

I am reminded of all the people I have met over the years. I have met a lot of people who seem to be genuine Satanists, who have a lot of money, who want to help other Satanists. But they only want to help Satanists if they can do it on the condition of being anonymous, because they are afraid of losing their job, or they are afraid their family might find out. What is disturbing about that is, some of these people we are talking about are grown men and women in their forties or fifties that are worried about their spouse finding out.

If you are a Satanist that can’t even deal with your own family and can't stand up for your religion with the people that are supposed to love you and supposed to accept you the way you are, what kind of representative are you of Satan? If you can't even deal with your own family life, how in the hell are you ever going to convince people that you deserve to be a Satanist? How in the hell are you ever going to convince anybody that Satanism is the right way of life for them if you can't even sort out your own problems long enough to be a

Satanist?

I am not putting these people down. I believe some of them genuinely believe in Satan, but Satanism is about being honest about who you are, and not letting yourself be controlled by fear or others who will not accept you. If you cannot even deal with the important people in your life, then you certainly cannot deal with the Lord of Darkness, because he will not let you hide. He will not let you hide away from yourself and let fear control you. Satan and the Demons make you face your fears. So if you want to be a Satanist and be successful at this religion, and get anything out of this, you have to be honest with your friends and family about who you are.

We are the minority religion. We cannot afford to have spineless people in our religion that let things just happen to them. Because there are so many of them, the Christians can afford to have a percentage of their membership be just bench-warmers, who just sit on the sidelines and let life pass them by. But we as Satanists are such a small minority that we have to have Satanists who sincerely stand up for the religion. The Christians have political power.

The Christians have social power. Satanists, as a general rule, have no power. We are considered the minority – the outcasts of society, and one of the reasons we are considered the outcasts is because we never stand up for ourselves. If we do not have pride in our religion and ourselves, and we are ashamed to admit that we are Satanists, then how can we expect to earn any respect for our god or our religion?

I am not suggesting that social acceptance is the be-all and end-all of Satanism. I feel that a lot of these people who are talking about "Satanic unification" and suggest that we should be politically correct so that society will accept us are naive, because it is never going to happen. This is more about you than it is what society thinks. You have to stand up for yourself so that you can have pride in yourself as a Satanist.

I feel the same way about Satanists who are afraid to admit they are Satanists as I do about people who are afraid to tell their family that they are gay. I do not understand how someone can know deep down inside that they are gay, and not have the guts to stand up and say, "I'm gay." How can you live a lie for years and years and years, and just accept it?

For me, it's just totally unbelievable that anybody could do that. I have always been the type of person who tells people if I believe in something. I told my mom and dad I was a Satanist when I was twelve. That's the way I am. I'm not saying that if you can't tell people you're a Satanist that you're wrong, I'm just saying you'll never be able to truly appreciate the freedom that Satanism has to offer.

In order to illustrate further why it is so important for us to stand up for our religion and ourselves let me give some examples. When I was doing a routine search for my local Satanism blog, I did a search on Satanism and what came up was a .pdf file from an event that was held in 2007 by Texas A&M Corpus Christi called "Camp on the Coast". In that handbook it stated that students were forbidden from wearing attire that depicted drug paraphernalia, gang signs, and Satanic imagery.

It occurred to me that in this day and age where we have religious freedom, where Satanism is a constitutionally protected religion, there are still people who lump our religion into the same category with gangs, illegal drug use, and criminal activity. All this even though the majority of people in Satanism are lawabiding citizens who have committed no crimes. I do not understand why university-educated people insist on putting a constitutionally protected religion in the same category with hoodlums and criminals, because we are not that.

Another thing that also occurred to me is that people constantly emphasize that our religion is a minority religion. They say that it has no real influence and only kooks and extremists believe in it, but that is because our religion is systematically discriminated against. Most Satanic organizations, regardless of location, cannot advertise in the phone book, newspapers, bulletin boards, bus benches, TV commercials, or radio commercials. If there is an organized effort to eliminate or at least limit people's freedom of speech, it is going to be a minority religion, regardless of what the ideas are, because you are preventing those people from exercising their freedom of speech.

The only exception to this organized effort to censor Satanists' freedom of speech is the internet, where all Satanists have freedom to express their ideas without interference from the government, at least for the time being. If it were not for the Internet, we would have even fewer people know about our religion. Any time people do not agree with what a religion says, they try to eliminate it. They do everything they can to try to make sure nobody is exposed to the ideas.

Despite these attempts to censor religious freedom of speech, people being curious by nature, they will try and find whatever information they can about a particular subject, no matter how much the government, the business community, or the media tries to limit the flow of that information. People want to know about things they do not understand, especially if it is taboo, and Satanism definitely fits that category.

I put a lot of the blame on the state of our religion and the way people perceive it on evangelical Christians, the media, and Satanists themselves. The media will claim anything that is remotely weird might be related to Satanism. If they find a dead cat mutilated on a lawn, they do not consider the possibility that a bunch of teenagers may have killed a cat because they had a grudge against someone who lived in the house where the cat was found. They automatically jump to the conclusion that it must be related to Satanism.

The reporting of stories involving animal mutilation usually goes something like this: "Cat found mutilated. Possibly related to Satanism," despite the fact that they have no evidence to indicate that the crime had anything to do with Satanism. Then the reporter will proceed to give credibility to his hypothesis that the cat mutilations were part of a Satanic ceremony by getting a quote from a so-called "occult expert."

Like in a story that I saw on my local news station's website that went something like this: "Captain So-and-So, Corpus Christi PD occult expert, says that the symbols discovered in a local park may suggest Satanic activity. This inverted cross on a black background is supposedly a symbol of "one nation under the Antichrist." I have never, in all my years of being a Satanist, seen that flag as a symbol of "one nation under the Antichrist."

I do not know where these people get their education from or where they get their designation as "occult experts," but it is clearly not accurate. It is also true that reporters often rely exclusively on police who have never been to a Satanic ritual and have probably never met a Satanist in person, and they let these so-called "occult experts" tell them what Satanism is about without doing their own research. Most reporters seem to have forgotten what a reporter's job is, and what the standards of reporting are supposed to be. Journalism students are commonly told in journalism school that you must have 2-3 sources of information to verify anything before you report it as fact. Sadly, the standards of journalism – along with police work – have clearly diminished greatly.

If you are a true journalist, you try to find the facts and report the truth. These people are clearly not journalists, because all they do is regurgitate what has been fed to them. Unfortunately, they do not do thorough research, and they do not study the subject of Satanism the way they should. This is due in large part to the fact that they consider stories about Satanism a waste of their time. Let's face it: it is not going to win them a Pulitzer Prize, and all they really care about is feeling special among their peers. They do not care about insignificant things like facts or details, because that would make them have to be real journalists.

It does not matter to them how people perceive Satanism, because they are just reporting a story, and they are just trying to sell papers or increase viewer ratings. Those of us who practice Satanism are affected by the stories they write because we have to deal with the consequences and the misconceptions people have about Satanism because of stories like theirs. The media has an interest in perpetuating negative stereotypes about Satanism because when something happens that involves Satanists they can sensationalize it, which will usually increase their profits, circulation, or ratings, if only temporarily.

The news and media business is so competitive these days that every newspaper, TV, and radio station is looking for something to give them an edge over the competition, and if they can figure out how to use Satanism to improve their competitive edge, they will use it. Plus, anything that involves people who the general public considers freaks or outcasts is going to get more attention from the press, because people are fascinated by the strange and unusual. And that is exactly how most people view those of us who worship Satan, whether we like it or not.

The second group of people I blame for the state of Satanism are the Satanists themselves, because Satanists have a tendency to come across with an attitude of, "Dude, I'll kick your ass!" or "I'm badass!" They wear the sunglasses, and they wear black, and they try to act all hard and they try to act like nothing can touch them, but as soon as the cops come and even remotely accuse them of something, they cower like a dog that has been beaten. As soon as they think the Child Protective Services is coming and might take their children because they have been falsely accused, they act like a bunch of spineless cowards.

They do not have any Satanic pride. They do not have any Satanic honor. I have seen otherwise good Satanists become fearful because a neighbor told the police that they were Satanists and they are afraid that their children might get taken away, and they act like slaves instead of Satanists with pride in their religion. They automatically just give up the fight. They do not go to the Child Protective Services and say, "I've done nothing wrong, and I'm not going to be afraid of you just because you work for the government, because Satanism is a constitutionally protected religion, and I will not be treated like a criminal." They do not go down to the school when somebody exposes their children to Christianity and say, "I don't want my children to learn this."

If you have nothing to hide, and you have nothing to fear, then why in the world would you act like a criminal? Why would you act like a slave? It is contrary to everything we believe in. This is not a traditionalist or modernist issue; this is a Satanism issue. It affects us all regardless of tradition. Every Satanist should stand up for themselves because if we do not stand up for ourselves, nobody else is going to. Nobody else gives a shit.

You have to start changing the way you think. You have to start changing the way you perceive yourself. You have to start seeing yourself as a servant of Satan, not just someone who is living their life day-to-day, surviving one moment to the next. Instead of looking at things from a mundane point of view, you need to start looking at them on a cosmic scale, and realize that your actions may have eternal consequences.

Most Christians do not put their career or their family before their duty to their god. They say to themselves, "I'm a Christian. I'm a servant of my god first." That is why they focus their life on their religion. That is why they dominate everything. That is why they spread their message better than we do. That is why they promote their religion better than we do, because when it comes to believing in their god, they do not just talk about it, they live by it – and many of them have died for it.

In the past, many of the forefathers of Satanism have been willing to sacrifice their life for Satan and his cause, but most Satanists today are unwilling to make a real sacrifice for their religion. Their idea of sacrifice is driving more than three hours to come to a ritual and paying fifty dollars for an information packet and membership card. How many Satanists do you know that have sacrificed their life for Satan?

How many Satanists do you know that are willing to be a martyr for their religion? Most of them are too busy worrying about, "Oh, god I hope nobody finds out I'm a Satanist! Oh, god I hope I don't lose my job! Oh, god I hope my wife doesn't find out I actually worship the Devil! Oh, god I hope nobody finds out I donated twenty bucks to that Satanic group on the internet!"

I am not suggesting to you that Satan requires us to be martyrs, I am just asking how many people you know that love Satan enough to put their lives on the line for his cause? This is something that every Satanist should take time to think about. We only have ourselves to blame for the state of our religion! Everybody thinks that I am so fanatical, everybody thinks I am so harsh, but can you honestly tell me that what I am saying is not true?

What I just said about Christianity – is it not true that they spread their message far better than we do? And why is that? They do this because their people work hard, because their people are disciplined, because their people believe in their god and in their message. What about us? Do none of us believe in our god and our religion enough to sacrifice anything? When are we going to start taking our religion seriously? That is part of the problem with Satanism: we wonder why people do not take us seriously (especially those of us who are traditionalists). We wonder why people treat our religion as such a joke.

They treat our religion as a joke because we as

Satanists treat it like it is a joke. We treat it like it is an afterthought, like it is something that we just do when we feel like it. We put on our Satanic image a few times a year at Solstices, Equinoxes, and Halloween, and we think that is good enough. We do not think of ourselves as Satanists 24/7, we just think of ourselves as Satanists when we put on our ritual robes and get ready for ritual, or we think of ourselves as Satanists when we have a party with other Satanists.

My friend has this problem: she does not see herself as a Satanist most of the time. She says, "I spend all this time taking care of the kids, or cleaning or working", and she forgets that she is a Satanist who happens to work a lot. You should never lose focus on the fact that you are a Satanist 24 hours a day, 7 days a week, and 365 days a year. Satanists are not made: it is something you are born to be or something you are not.

If you are a Satanist, and that is your destiny, that should be your top priority in life. As Satanists, we should not worry about what society, the police, the media, the government, or anyone else thinks about us. We should be more concerned about what Satan and his Demons think about us, because it is them we are going to spend our eternity with.

CHAPTER VIII

SATANISM, FAMILY, AND CHILDREN

MANY people argue that you should never force your religion upon your children, and that children should be allowed to make their own choice about what they believe. I wholeheartedly agree. In our religion, we do not believe a child can be forced to accept Satan. As a matter of fact, we believe if a parent were to force the religion down a child's throat, they would be breaking the very law of Satan.

Having said that, however, I believe children should be exposed to Satanism and Satanic ritual at an early age. This will give them a more accurate view of Satan and Satanism, and they will not have the negative stereotypes and prejudices that the people who have been raised in a strictly Christian society would have about the religion. A child can not truly accept Satan until they understand what free will is, and until they make that choice on their own, without being coerced, they cannot be considered a Satanist. For every child, the age where they understand the concept of free will is different, and they should be judged on a case-by-case basis.

Many parents ask whether they should baptize their child before they are old enough to understand it, and the answer is no, absolutely not. A child should not receive a full Satanic baptism until they have expressed an interest in receiving a baptism on their own and they show a clear indication that they understand free will and the importance of the choice they are about to make.

A parent should test them and make sure they understand Satanism. If the parent is satisfied that the child is old enough and has a full understanding of the commitment they are about to make, a baptism can be performed.

Prior to performing a full baptism, a parent can perform a Satanic blessing upon the child, asking for Satan's guidance and protection if they so choose, which is something I highly recommend for any child, but especially if they have two Satanic parents. This ceremony should be performed the first night the child is home from the hospital, and should probably be performed by the father, because he will probably be the one in the best condition to perform a ritual.

Remember, this is not dedicating them to Satan or making a pact with Satan. This is asking for Satan's guidance and protection to be upon the child. Only the child can make a pact with Satan, when the child is old enough to make that choice.

There are rare occasions where the parent has made a pact to dedicate the child to Satan's service before the child is conceived or while the mother is still pregnant. But these are exceedingly rare cases, and since these arrangements are usually made at the request of the spirits, they are unique, and the conditions vary greatly from case to case. For this reason, I feel it is imprudent to comment further upon these special cases.

Also, parents should bear in mind that children want to do the things that their parents do and want to be like them, so they will often copy their parents' behavior and want to be a part of rituals. But just because a child shows an interest in being like their parents does not mean they have a genuine, heartfelt interest in Satanism and are ready to make the choice to be Satanists. Many children want to be involved in what their parents are involved in because they are seeking parental praise and acceptance, and parents should not get overly excited and start pushing Satanism on the child, because it is likely that the child is just copying parental behavior.

Children should be encouraged to engage in religious activities if they show an interest, but parents should not get discouraged if the interest in religion seems to be a phase. This is because many things that you teach them when they are young, they will think about when they are older and mature enough to understand them, and it is very possible that their interest will be rekindled later in life. Once the parents have decided whether or not they are going to ask for a Satanic blessing on their child, the next question that they ask is inevitably going to be "How do I start teaching my children about Satanism?"

The easiest way to start exposing your children to Satanic philosophy is to take the *Al-Jilwah* and turn it into a children's story. Many mothers and fathers, if they have had children before, are already experienced at breaking down complex ideas into simple stories or parables. It should be very simple to turn the *Al-Jilwah* or other sacred texts into simple stories that help the children understand the nature and personality of Satan. Explaining to the children the relationship between the Christian god and Satan by using a very simple story that the children can relate to is also a good idea. For example:

"One day, Baphomet had a fight with the Christian god, and the Christian god got mad at Baphomet. And Baphomet got mad at the Christian god, and decided to leave his house and move into his own house, which Baphomet called Hell. Eventually some of Baphomet's friends (the fallen angels), like Abbadon, decided to go live with Baphomet because they felt that the Christian god had been mean to Baphomet."

You can get the idea from this example. If you are an experienced parent, you are probably better at explaining things in a way that a child can understand than I am, because I don't have any children. Even though I don't have children, I have been around enough Satanic parents who have used these methods successfully to teach their children about Satanism and its philosophy to know that they do work effectively.

If you are particularly artistic, you can illustrate these stories and allow children to color in the pictures. If you would like to teach the children about magickal correspondences, you can use the tarot cards as a guide to create flashcards that show the children a symbol of air, for example, and list the meanings of that symbol. Or, create a tarot card that shows a symbol for Mars, and teach them the attributions associated with Mars, etc.

The best time to start teaching them this is when they are learning their ABC's. This serves two purposes: first, it gives them an understanding of the elements and the planets and how they affect us and our universe in a magickal sense, and it also prevents them from having to struggle to learn it when they get older. It is best to teach them magickal attributions when they are at an age where they can learn it much faster. By the time they become teenagers, it will be almost second nature to them.

If they decide to be Satanists, and get seriously involved in ceremonial magick, they will have a head start compared to people who come to the occult later in life. And if they decide not to be Satanists, at the very least they will be able to understand astrological and magickal concepts that will help them relate to people of alternative religious faiths, which might help them when they are older, depending on what career they choose. Whether they become a Satanist or not, this information may prove useful later in life.

The only downside to teaching them about magick and Satanism before they have made a commitment to Satan is if they rebel against their family and become a born-again Christian. There is always the possibility that they will become an evangelist and use the information you have taught them against our faith and us.

Another way that you can expose children to Satanic ideas without having to force it down their throat is through the observance of Satanic holidays. The two that lend themselves best to helping reinforce Satanic ideas in a way that children can understand them are Halloween and Winter Solstice (or Saturnalia).

Halloween for the most part, especially in the United States, is already a holiday that has activities that are directed towards children. If you take your children out trick-or-treating, it is a perfect time to explain how costumes and masks were used in ancient pagan religious ceremonies. When the children come home with their candy, you can explain to them how sweets and other food offerings were used to keep spirits friendly to the people in their houses, or to welcome ancestors. Most activities associated with Halloween have some pagan origin.

So, as you are engaging in these traditional activities, you can give your children a history lesson. With a little time and effort, you should be able to find books that explain the pagan traditions behind various Halloween and Winter Solstice activities.

I would like to point out something before I move on

to discussing Winter Solstice: in our particular tradition, we consider Traditional Satanism a form of paganism, so we consider pagan traditions to be part of Satanism. It should also be noted that we believe that certain Demons are also pagan deities. Since we regard Traditional Satanism as a pagan religion, we see no conflict with teaching children the pagan origins of these holidays.

Next let us discuss Winter Solstice, Yule, or Saturnalia. There is not much that is Christian about it except for the name Christmas. Christmas trees, yule logs, mistletoe, and holly berries all originally had their place in Norse pagan rituals. The evergreen tree represented the return of spring and acted as a reminder that the crops would soon grow again. Yule logs were burned to symbolize the triumph of the sun god over the darkness of winter. Kissing under the mistletoe was part of an old fertility ritual, and holly berries were used to feed the gods.

Even the custom of gift-giving was practiced by the Romans as a part of their Saturnalia celebrations. If you move everything that you did on Christmas to the date of the Winter Solstice, and you're practicing the traditions on the day that they were intended to be practiced, then all you have to do is teach the children the true origins and history of the holiday.

DEALING WITH RELATIVES WHO ARE WITHOUT

Every Satanist, at some point or another, will have to deal with relatives who are not Satanists, who will try to give them advice about how to raise their children. And if the relatives know they are Satanists – unless the parents are very strong – they will try to influence the parents not to teach their children about Satanism. So the parents of a Satanic child must be very strong and very firm in their convictions, and make the necessary sacrifices to ensure that their children are not left with relatives who might undermine what the parents are trying to teach the child.

For example, young parents may be desperate for some time alone together, so they may decide "it won't hurt if we let grandma or grandpa take care of the baby for the evening," even though they know that grandma or grandpa are Christian. And most grandparents or relatives, if they are Christian, will slip in an occasional Bible verse or some mention of Jesus, no matter how much they say they would not do it.

That is the primary mission of a Christian, to try and convert people who are not of their faith to their faith. It has been programmed into them like a machine. It is far better, if you are a Satanist, to leave your child with someone who is neutral than with someone who is Christian, no matter if they are a relative or not.

Now do not misunderstand me: I am not suggesting that you should leave your children with someone who is neutral if you have a Satanist who is available to baby-sit them. But since most people do not have Satanists who live near them that they would trust with their children, they are usually left with the dilemma of trying to make a decision between Christian relatives and someone who is neutral, such as a friend. And I would always pick the friend or someone who is neutral over someone who is Christian. Parents must always be on guard, because it will be a constant struggle to try and keep members of the family who are Christian from trying to influence the children with their religious ideas.

SATANIC CHILDREN AND SCHOOL

Once the children are old enough to go to school, this gives rise to a whole new set of issues those parents must think about and deal with. A critical decision they must make is whether they are going to send the child to public school, private school, or educate the child at home. The benefit of raising a child in the United States is that the Supreme Court has determined that there should be a separation between church and state, which means that teachers and administrators are not allowed to teach children religion in school.

This does not mean, however, that your child will not occasionally encounter the rogue teacher who will decide it is their personal mission to be a crusader for the Christian god, and will inevitably try to teach your child about how virtuous the Christian faith is. But compared to many European countries, where religious assemblies and religious classes are mandatory, unless the parents put it in writing specifically asking the headmaster to exclude their children from those classes (which does not always work), the American school system is more friendly towards alternative religious points of view.

Private schools are usually not the best options for Satanic parents who want to send their children to get a high-quality education, because most private schools are based in Judeo-Christian teachings, not to mention the added expense of tuition which many parents cannot afford. There is nothing more irritating than paying a lot of extra money to have someone ram religious teachings that are contrary to your own down your child's throat, no matter how good the education may be.

In my opinion, home-school would be the best option for those parents who are serious about instilling Satanic values into their children, as well as giving them the best education possible. Unlike Christians, we do not have a Satanic home-school association, but thankfully, there are secular home-school associations where you can get educational assistance without a religious overtone. With a little bit of research, you can find a great deal of information on the internet about secular home-school associations, and you can make a decision about which ones suit you and your child best.

It is unfortunate that far too many Satanists take a lackadaisical attitude towards our religion and have not already established organizations like these. This is an excellent example, in my opinion, that Satanists do not take Satanism seriously. If they did, they would not want their children exposed to Christian ideas, and they would establish organizations to ensure that their children were taught in an environment that is free from ideas that contradict the Satanic religion. One of my dreams is to see a Satanic home-school association at some time in the future.

I would like to give one last piece of advice before you make a decision about whether you are going to send your children to school. It is probably best, in order to prevent yourself a lot of unnecessary headaches, to teach the children when they are very young to use an alternative name for Satan. A good substitute is "Baphomet." This is because when they go to school, young children do not realize the stigma attached to the name "Satan." While some people may be familiar with the name Baphomet, the majority of them will not be. Also, the name Baphomet does not have the negative connotations that Satan does, and you are far less likely to get a call from teachers or Child Protective Services if they overhear the child using the name Baphomet.

Now I am not suggesting that if you feel strongly about using the name Satan with your children that you are doing anything wrong. But you must bear in mind that if your children use the name Satan at school, you are going to be getting calls from your local teachers and possibly Child Protective Services. If you are willing to deal with all that, and accept the consequences that may come from your children talking about Satan and Satanism at the most inopportune times, then I say more power to you. I have a great deal of respect for people who take this route, because that is what I would do if I had children of my own.

ABORTION

No chapter on Satanism, family, and children would be complete without a discussion on abortion. In my view, to abort a child who has Satanic blood in them is considered the highest form of disrespect to Satan. If the child has Satanic blood in them, then they are considered sacred, and would never be aborted.

I would even feel safe in saying to you that most female Traditional Satanists that I know would not abort a child, even if they had been raped. The child is still considered sacred, because of the mere fact that it has the mother's Satanic blood flowing through its veins. And let's face it, after all, it is not the child's fault that the father chose to rape the mother.

In the tradition I follow, we believe that children are a gift from Satan, and that while children may be genetically the products of their parents, they are not truly ours. They are given to us by Satan, and we have the responsibility of raising them, and teaching them, and making them the best people they can be, and guiding them on their path in the Satanic religion if they choose to serve Satan.

ADOPTION

Some people will ask whether or not they should adopt children if they are unable to have them, and whether or not an adopted child can and should be raised in the Satanic religion. Up until this point I have discussed children who have at least one Satanic parent, but I want to stress a point: Satan can choose anyone he wishes, regardless of whether they are related to Satanists by blood or not. It is not impossible to believe that Satan could influence events so that a Satanic couple who wanted to adopt a child is led to someone who is destined to become a Satanist. After all, most of us who are Satanists and have felt Satan's call are not Satanists by blood.

The reason that our group emphasizes the importance of bloodline is because people who have Satanic parents usually exhibit signs of heightened spiritual awareness and psychic ability that far exceed those who do not have Satanic parents. And if given the choice, a Satanist with two Satanic parents is far more desirable than a Satanist with one Satanic parent.

That is not to say that children who only have one Satanic parent are not important or not valuable in the eyes of Satan, or should be treated as subhuman by a Satanic Coven. It just means that those who have both a Satanic mother and a Satanic father are likely to have, again, a heightened psychic awareness that exceeds those who do not. They are therefore likely to have a much easier time connecting and communicating with Satan and Demons, because based on our experience, Satan honors those who carry on a hereditary bloodline.

It is also important to point out that another reason why bloodline is important is because we consider Satanists to be a race unto themselves, not merely followers of a religion. We will be discussing this in more detail in another chapter.

Being a parent is one of the most important things an individual can do. And being a Satanic parent is even more important, because not only are you preserving your genetic code and your Demonic spiritual essence, but you are literally preserving the very future of our race and our religion, and there is nothing more important to Satanism than that. By passing down our religious traditions and teachings to our children, we are not only preserving our religion and our race, but we are laying the groundwork for a future that will have cosmic implications.

CHAPTER IX

TEENAGE SATANISTS

I have always believed that children and teenagers are the future of the Satanic religion. I believe they are the future because they are not already programmed with preconceived notions about who Satan is and what his motivations are. They have not bought into the lies and the misconceptions about Satan like adults have, because they have not had time yet to be programmed by the Abrahamic faiths.

And even though there may be a few that have already been brainwashed to some degree by the Christians because their parents are involved in some form of Christianity, most of them have not been influenced by Christianity enough that it has become a festering disease within their soul. They can easily be redirected into a more positive frame of mind and religious worship.

Unfortunately, there has not been enough attention paid to teenage Satanists by the Satanic community, and as such, many of them form their own teenage Covens without any knowledge from older, more experienced Satanists, and this is what usually leads them into trouble. When these Covens are formed, they are usually led or founded by people who know slightly more than the members they have selected to be a part of their group.

Usually these leaders are more concerned with their own personal power or their own ego than they are with building a genuine Satanic group. It should be noted that these types of leaders are not limited to teenage Covens. There are just as many adults in Satanism that have the same motivations.

The difference is, no matter how much the leader of the group may be obsessed with obtaining personal power, most adults are mature enough to restrain themselves from doing anything that would get the Coven into trouble with the law. This is not to say that some teenagers are incapable of understanding this, but they are more likely to get drawn into criminal activities due to peer pressure than adults would be.

That is why I have always suggested that if teenagers want to form their own Coven, they have an adult mentor. A good mentor can advise them about their curriculum, make sure that they stay on the right track, and keep them from getting involved in things detrimental to both them and the Satanic community.

Many adults who may read this, if they are not Satanists, would have a problem with me suggesting that a teen Coven have an adult mentor. The reason many parents would have a problem with this is because they have this idea that adult Satanists are out to molest their children or get them involved in underage pornography, but Satanists as a general rule have no desire to do that.

There are bad people in every religion, and our religion is no exception. It would be a lie for me to say that there are no pedophiles in our religion, because there are pedophiles in every religion, but just because we are Satanists does not mean there are more child molesters per capita than any other religion.

Because people have bought into the stereotypes perpetuated by books, the media, and films, they tend to believe that people who worship the Devil are somehow more prone to engage in illicit activities with children than any other religion, but that is simply not true. There is absolutely no evidence that those who worship Satan are prone to engage in pedophilia more than the followers of any other religion.

I would argue with parents who are reluctant to let their children talk to adult Satanists by pointing out that whenever children engage in criminal activities or other things their parents disapprove of, it is usually because they are talking to someone who is the same age as they are. This friend of theirs may just happen to be involved in Satanism. And more often than not, their Satanist friend has very little experience in the religion.

Most teenagers, because they have not had the experience that results from practicing Satanism for years, do not stop to take the time to think about the consequences of what they do. An adult Satanist might make them stop and think about the consequences, and because they respect the adult because they know them to be a serious Satanist, more often than not, they will listen. I know this to be true because I have had teenagers listen to me and take my advice before they listen to their parents, because I am a Satanist and their parents are not.

Their parents, because they are not Satanists themselves, do not understand where the teenager is coming from. They do not understand what their son or daughter believes, and they have difficulty finding common ground and understanding how to relate to the child. Whereas an adult Satanist, because they share the same beliefs, can tell the teenager how to deal with any situation that arises from a Satanic perspective.

Because many parents fear that adult Satanists have other motives besides teaching the children about Satanism, they are reluctant to have their children speak to adult Satanists. They fail to understand that regardless of what they do, if the child is determined to become a Satanist and learn about Satanism, they are going to do it whether they like it or not.

And if they are speaking with an adult Satanist, then the parents can monitor what is being taught to their child and ask any questions if they should have any concerns about what their child is learning. I myself have no problem speaking to people's parents, and I am more than willing to speak to any parent who has an interest in Satanism and explain to them what I am going to teach their children.

In my experience, the average offline group of Satanists, whether adult or teen, usually consists of three to five members, and in the case of teenage Covens, the average time they have been involved in Satanism is one to three years. Usually in the case of teenage Covens, it is the leader who has been involved anywhere from one to three years. Most of the other members of the group have only been involved in Satanism for one to two years at the most, and were usually brought into Satanism by the "leader."

Most teenage groups do not practice an established form of Satanism, whether it's traditional or modern. Most teenage Covens are one of two types.

The first type of Coven is relatively benign. This type of Coven is the type of group that is more like a fraternity, where the group members are more interested in partying, smoking dope, and getting laid than they are with worshiping Satan. Satan is merely the catalyst for their behavior. In other words, they want to rebel against their parents and society and experiment with alternative lifestyles, and what better excuse can there be than "the Devil made me do it?" They use the Devil and his religion a way to justify their behavior.

The second type of teenage Coven is more dangerous, because most of the time the philosophies upon which these Covens are based are those which are advantageous to the leader and assist them in manipulating their subordinates. Usually they follow this leader because of his or her personal charisma and perceived knowledge of Satanism.

Their philosophy is usually a mixture of different ideas from different magickal or Satanic orders that have been adapted or reinterpreted by their leader. The reason the philosophy is usually a mixture of different magickal and Satanic groups is because these types of Satanists have not been involved in Satanism long enough to have any practical experience, so they base their philosophy largely on what they read instead of real-world Satanism.

There is something I want to say before we go any further: adult Satanists should not dismiss a teenager because of their age. I believe that there are rare teenagers out there who are exceptional, and who truly have the maturity and the desire to serve Satan, but I believe they are rare. It is also interesting that the majority of Traditional Satanists (Devil Worshipers) usually had their first experience that convinced them Satan does exist anywhere from early childhood to midteens.

TEENAGERS WITH FAMILIES HOSTILE TO SATANISM

Many teenagers who get involved in Satanism will inevitably be confronted with having to make some serious choices when their parents find out they are a

Satanist. If their parents or guardians are not tolerant of Satanism, more often that not, this difference of religious opinion will escalate into a serious family dispute, and teenagers often feel that the only solution is to run away from home. As drastic as this may seem, it is a choice that teenagers are faced with all too often.

I received a call once from a young kid who said, "My parents don't like the fact that I'm a Satanist. My parents think that it's stupid. My parents think that I'm crazy for believing in it. What should I do? I want to run away from home." I told the kid that he should not run away from home because he was only 15 years old. He only had a few more years to put up with it, and if he was strong in his faith and truly believed in it, then he could hold out for a few more years.

It was a very difficult situation to deal with because he was upset enough that he was crying, and he was telling me that if he did not run away from home that he would kill himself because he just couldn’t take it anymore. He said all he wanted to do was worship Satan and practice his religion freely, and his parents just did not understand and refused to allow him to.

I never found out what happened, because the kid never called me back. When I hung up with him, he seemed to be in a much better mood, and he said that what I said made sense, but he still didn't know if he would be able to deal with it.

If he had been talking to another teen Satanist they probably would have said, "Yeah dude, fuck that bitch, fuck your mom. Just run away, dude – do whatever the hell you want." But I did not tell him that. I told him that a strong Satanist would bear with the situation, and wait until they were in a better position to have control over their own life. There was no need to rock the boat because he only had about three more years before he would be able to make decisions for himself, and it would really serve no purpose. And besides, how can you truly concentrate on your religious studies and becoming a better Satanist when you are out on the street with no place to live and no food to eat?

Another thing that teenagers often ask is, “How should I go about worshiping Satan if my parents don't allow me to practice in my home?” First and foremost, it is not necessary to have ritual equipment in order to build a relationship with Satan and Demons. Simple prayer works very well, as long as it is sincere and you are honest with Satan and the Demons about what you are asking for. To some people, this may seem very Christian, but you must keep in mind that Christians did not invent prayer. To illustrate my point, here is a portion of a prayer from the Egyptian Book of the Dead:

"O you four baboons who sit in the bow of the Bark of Re, who raise up the truth to the Lord of All, who judge poor and rich, who propitiate the gods with the breath of your mouths, who give god's-offerings to the gods and invocation-offerings to the spirits, who live on truth and gulp down truth, whose hearts have no lies, who detest falsehood: expel my evil, grip hold of my falsehood, and I will have no guilt in respect of you. Grant that I may open up the tomb, that I may enter into Rosetjau, and that I may pass by the secret portals of the West. There shall be given to me a shens-cake, a jug of beer and a persen-loaf, just like those spirits who go in and out in Rosetjau." (Spell 126)

Just like with any mortal relationship, the easiest way to build a connection with someone is to have a sincere heart-to-heart conversation with them, and that is, after all, what prayer is in its most simplistic form: a hearttoheart conversation with your gods.

If your parent or guardian does not allow you to do prayer rituals and you have the desire to perform rituals to Satan, here is an excellent alternative. Go to a public park in a secluded area, find a solid surface such as a picnic table, a park bench, or other similar structure, and lay a black piece of material over it. Consecrate the cloth as your altar so that it can be used in future rituals.

Also, if you are relatively artistic, it might be a good idea to draw an inverted pentagram or symbol of Baphomet on your cloth. You can use the image as something to focus on while you are doing your rituals to get you in the right frame of mind. If you are in an outdoor location where wind tends to be a problem, you can buy oil candles that will not go out when the wind blows.

When picking a location, it should be somewhere that you will not be disturbed during your ritual, and has spiritual significance to you, or at least feels like it is an appropriate place to do your ritual. For tips on how to put together a basic ritual, see the chapter entitled "Daily Ritual Practice".

ADVICE FOR TEENS WHOSE PARENTS FORCE THEM TO ATTEND CHURCH

The first thing you should do is anoint yourself, if you have the oil to do it, and ask Satan and his Demons to protect you against the spirit of the Judeo-Christian god and his angels. If you don't have any oil, a simple prayer will suffice. Once you do this, if you are going to have to go to church, synagogue, or mosque against your will, try to think of the most effective counter-arguments to the arguments made by the ministers, rabbis, or imams against your religion.

You can either look at this time as a negative experience, or you can look at it as an opportunity to learn as much as you can about the enemy and his followers. This will make you more able to hold your own in religious debates with followers of other faiths. It also allows you to explain more effectively the differences between the philosophy and morality of Satanism and the Abrahamic religious traditions.

CHAPTER X

SOLITARY PRACTICE VS JOINING A COVEN

A lot of people are afraid to get involved in Satanism with a group because they are afraid something bad is going to happen, or they are afraid they are going to be drawn into something very negative. Unfortunately, in many cases, if you are not extremely careful, it is very likely that you will be drawn into a very negative environment.

Let's be honest: there are many individuals who run Satanic groups who are not motivated by a true desire to further the Satanic religion. They are motivated by their own personal desires, which usually have very little to do with the actual worship of Satan.

Most people are reluctant to get involved with a group because they have heard horror stories about group leaders who manipulate their members, either for money or sex, and you will certainly not get any argument from me that this does not happen. Sadly, it happens far too often than most Satanists would like to admit.

But as horrible as these experiences may be, if you allow the potential for a negative experience to discourage you from joining a Coven, you are missing out on an experience that cannot be matched. You cannot substitute it for anything, and having a true group experience has many positive aspects to it. If you join a genuine group made up of dedicated Satanists, then a group experience is truly unique and the things you learn are not things you can recreate through solitary practice.

Some people choose to be solitary practitioners because they are afraid of going public or even sharing their beliefs with other people. But I think once they get over their initial fear, they will find that they really had a deep-seated desire to be part of a group, and socialize with other Satanists like themselves. There are legitimate reasons to do solitary rituals, and some of the reasons are when you work on yourself as an individual – for instance, if you want to concentrate on developing your psychic ability or on a particular meditation technique.

I always encourage people to design their own rituals, but I also encourage them to get involved and study with a group and do group rituals, because if you don't do that, you're not getting the complete experience. You will not have a full understanding of what it means to be a Satanist, and I do not care how self-reliant or knowledgeable you think you are, you cannot truly call yourself a Satanist without understanding the dynamics of a Coven setting. Only individuals who have never been a part of a serious Coven would be foolish enough to say that they are complete without having had a group experience. It's not only an ignorant statement to make, but it is a colossal monument to one's stupidity. Some of this is not just my opinion, it's a fact.

Another area where there is a great deal of confusion is with the use of the term initiation. People talk about initiation, but they do not really understand what initiation is. Many individuals do not make the distinction between the different types of initiation. There are two distinct types: the first, and one most often referred to by occult authors, is the self-initiation, which is a process of personal growth through meditation or other techniques to develop one's spiritual, magickal, or psychic abilities. This type of initiation process is the one best suited for solitary rituals because the techniques focus on developing and strengthening the individual in some way, and in order to achieve this you must be able to focus on yourself and what you are trying to achieve without distraction.

In this chapter, I am focusing more on the group initiation process rather than the initiation of the individual. Group initiation happens when each member of the group goes through the same trials and experiences as every other member of the group, thereby creating a spiritual, as well as emotional, bond between the members of the Coven. This type of initiation helps bind you to the people that you are working with. It is something that will change you if it is done correctly.

There are things you can gain from a group ritual that you cannot gain from a personal ritual. For one, when a group of people is focused on a single idea, there is a power, there is a presence that can be felt that you cannot experience when doing a ritual on your own. Also, if you are a member of a group who actually cares about each other, then you have camaraderie and a brotherhood that cannot be replaced.

That doesn't mean people are going to get along all the time or that they are always going to be buddy-buddy, but there is a bond there between you and the group that you have been working with. That bond is unique to the individuals involved in the group, because you have been through similar rituals and through similar situations and you have all worked together in a ritual environment to achieve both your spiritual and magickal ends.

By doing these things together, it creates a bond that you cannot sever. It will make you a stronger person, and it will give you a sense of community that you have not had. So again, if you are a Traditional Satanist who is a solitary practitioner, do not discount group rituals, and do not rule them out, because as I said before, if you do, you are missing out on part of what it means to be a Satanist.

CHAPTER XI

THE LACK OF HONOR, LOYALTY AND RESPECT IN THE SATANIC COMMUNITY

IF you spend any time talking to other Satanists, you will eventually come across Traditional Satanists who will say, "Satan is my everything, Satan is my master, I'll do anything for Satan. I would never do anything to go against him." Then they proceed to put curses on other Traditional Satanic organizations and their leaders without thinking about the consequences of their actions or the possible long-term effects they may have on the Satanic community as a whole. They are simply mad about something that group or one of its leaders said about them or one of their friends.

People do not ever think about Satan first – they think about themselves first. All these people that say, " Satan means everything to me" will belittle each other over the simplest, stupidest things without thinking for one second that they might be undermining Satan's will by doing so. I have seen people curse each other because a person is dating the other person's ex-girlfriend or ex-boyfriend.

You do not put curses on your fellow Traditional Satanists just because you are pissed off at them. Any real Traditional Satanist that is thinking more about Satan's cause than their personal problems would know this. There are prohibitions in Traditional Satanism about putting curses on your fellow brothers and sisters in Satan. In our particular tradition, we do not put curses on a fellow Satanist, even if they say or do something against us. We do not attack our own brothers and sisters. We worry about how it might interfere with Satan’s will, and if people were really interested in doing Satan's will, they would think about him first instead of themselves.

Far too many people have lost an understanding of what it means to have honor, what it means to have integrity, what it means to respect your mentors, your High Priests and your High Priestesses, and your Coven, and the oaths that you have made. I will be the first to admit that I have in the past been guilty of doing some of those very things, in the sense that I have judged other people and have not always been the easiest person to work with.

I also will admit to you that I have taken a great deal of time to think about that. I've taken time to think about what I'm doing and what I'm saying, and how it might undermine what Satan has in store for the Satanic community, or how I might be interfering with somebody else's work that Satan has set for them. Nowadays I tend to have a more reserved, more tempered viewpoint than I used to have.

There are many Satanists that I do not particularly care for, but one thing I would never do is put a curse on a fellow Satanist, because I have personal standards. And there is a higher power that I answer to, and that is the one we are supposed to be serving, and we have no right to interfere magically with another Satanic organization if we do not know what is going on. We have no way of knowing what that organization is doing, what those leaders have been instructed to do, and we may disrupt something by cursing them. So despite how angry I may be, I would never put a curse on another Satanist.

Another issue I have is that people do not show proper respect to their High Priest and High Priestess, although they talk about how much they respect them. I have two people that I consider to have authority over me and can tell me what to do. They are my High Priest and High Priestess.

And have I been angry at them? Yes. Have I been upset with some of the decisions they have made? Yes. But would I dare ever talk about them in a negative way? Would I ever belittle my mentors or the people that I respect in public? No, because you don't do that. In traditional Covens you do not disrespect your priest, your priestess, your mentor, or those who helped make you who you are. That is something that has been lost in the Traditional Satanic community.

Many Satanists seem almost incapable of understanding that if you do not respect your High Priest and High Priestess to keep the commitments that you have made to them and your Coven, you should not have been calling them your High Priest and High Priestess in the first place. You will see Satanists who will insult the people who brought them into the religion. You will see Satanists who will speak badly about their former mentors, because they do not like something they said.

Even if I left the group I am currently with – even if I was upset and I parted ways with them – you would never see me utter a single derogatory word in public against my High Priest and High Priestess. This is because I respect them enough that even if I were to part ways with them, I would not do it. This is out of respect for them, Satan, and the oaths that I have made.

When most of us became Traditional Satanists, we acknowledged that there was a higher power, a higher authority that was above us named Satan, and his Demons both named and nameless. And we knew and understood that from time to time we would have to do things that were not necessarily our will, but what was best for the Satanic community. That is what makes us different from LaVeyans.

That is what makes us Traditional Satanists, and if you throw that reverence and respect for Satan out the window, and only do what you want, then you may as well not be a Satanist at all. This community has become a community where we will turn on a brother for nothing. We will go out of our way to destroy a brother or sister not because they have done something against Satan, not because they have done something against the community, but because they have done something against us personally. We pay no attention to what it might mean for the Satanic community as a whole.

I know that some of you are probably reading this and thinking, "So what are you saying Nero, that we should turn the other cheek when another Traditional Satanist does something to us?" No, I am not saying that. You should step back from it and think about whether the petty differences that you have with this person are worth undermining Satan's will.

Another problem that I often see is that many individuals, when they join a Satanic Coven or group, do not join with the intention of having a long-term relationship with the Coven they are joining. They join with the intention of learning as much as they can, as fast as they can, so they can take what they have learned and start their own Coven.

Many of these individuals are not motivated to start their own Covens because they have a true desire to serve Satan. They start their own Covens because they have a desire to be important, to be somebody, and give themselves titles that mean absolutely nothing because they were not given to them by Satan. For example, you will often see people on the internet with long magickal titles that are linguistically and magickally incorrect that are basically saying – in a long-winded way – "I am Brother So-and-So, Master of the Universe and Lord of All."

There is no mention of or reverence for Satan in these titles at all. No one ever seems to come to a Coven with the desire to help build a tradition. It always seems to be about them, and never about Satanism, and if we as a Traditional Satanic community keep acting this way, and keep having the attitude that nothing is more important than us and our desires, then there will not be any tradition for future generations to follow.

Your first commitment is to Satan, to be loyal to him and to do his will. And if what you are doing just because you are more worried about you undermines his work, then what kind of Traditional Satanist are you, and can you truly call yourself a child and servant of Satan?

CHAPTER XII

MODERN SATANISM, ANTON LAVEY, AND THE SATANIC BIBLE

ANTON LAVEY

NO matter what your opinions are of Anton LaVey, it is true that he has made great contributions to the Satanic religion, and the contributions that he has made cannot be overlooked. There are many things that LaVey should be given credit for.

The most important one, in my opinion, is that he brought the *Al-Jilwah* to the attention of the public, which I personally believe was Satan's will. It should be noted that LaVey's version which appears in *The Satanic Rituals* has been altered from the original. Certain words have been changed and small portions were omitted. The original text of the *Al-Jilwah* has been included in this book for reference.

Secondarily, he packaged the Satanic philosophy in such a simple way that even a person who is not very occult-oriented can understand it. It can not be denied that LaVey was a marketing genius. His public performance of Satanic rituals, such as the baptism of his daughter Zeena LaVey in 1967, are a clear example of LaVey's understanding of public interest in things that are out-of-the-ordinary, which assured his place in the history of Satanism and proved his marketing savvy.

The one area of *The Satanic Bible* that has its own

unique style is the rituals. While the structure may not be original, the way in which they are worded and the style in which they are performed is uniquely LaVey. And as much as I hate to admit it, LaVey's rituals are effective to some degree.

However, having said that, I will not give LaVey credit for things he does not deserve. It is a popular misconception in the Satanic community that LaVey coined the term "Satanism"; obviously, he did not. Evidence of this can be found in a book by Montague Summers called *The History of Witchcraft and Demonology*, which was published in 1927, before Anton LaVey was even born. In this book, Summers uses the terms "Satanism", "Traditional Satanism" and "Devilworship" interchangeably to describe those who worshiped Satan as a literal entity, which means the Church of Satan's claims that they created the term "Satanism" are clearly false.

LaVey's tendency to take credit for things he neither wrote nor created does not stop with the term "Satanism." The "Book of Satan" in *The Satanic Bible* is clearly a plagiarism of "Might is Right" by Ragnar Redbeard, originally published in 1890. Conclusive evidence of LaVey's blatant plagiarism can be found in the "Book of Satan," which lifts entire sentences wordfor- word from Redbeard's book.

I also will not give LaVey credit for being the originator of the Satanic philosophy and way of life, because the principles of Crowley's writings, such as "Liber Oz," are very similar to those you see in *The Satanic Bible*. And it is clear that LaVey was influenced by these ideas, whether he admits it or not. Crowley's statement that "there is no god but man" in "Liber Oz" shows that this text had an influence on LaVey's philosophy.[14] This is one example among many in "Liber Oz" that seems to show clear links between the teachings of Crowley and the philosophy of LaVey.

I would like to point out that I do not give Crowley credit for being the originator of these ideas either; I believe that the originator of these ideas of man having the potential of being godlike and thinking for himself originated with Lucifer. "But of the fruit of the tree which is in the midst of the garden, God hath said, 'Ye shall not eat of it, neither shall ye touch it, lest ye die.' And the serpent said unto the woman, 'Ye shall not surely die: For God doth know that in the day ye eat thereof, then your eyes shall be opened, and ye shall be as gods, knowing good and evil." (Genesis 3:3-5)

While I realize that some diehard Satanists may find it somewhat disconcerting that I use Biblical verses throughout this book to support my beliefs, I am just trying to illustrate that the belief that mankind could become equal with the gods or god goes back to antiquity. And as a consequence, this certain idea cannot be attributed to modern occult authors.

This verse is particularly relevant because the spirit that delivered the "*Book of the Law*" to Crowley used very similar phrases in Chapter II. For example: "I am

14 The fact that Crowley uses the phrase "there is no god but man" is somewhat confusing, considering that the inspiration for this Liber was clearly the "Book of the Law", which Crowley attributes to Aiwass, which he associates with Satan/Lucifer, the devil, in Magick Book Four. One of the things that makes Crowley so perplexing is that he associates Aiwass with his higher self, or his Holy Guardian Angel, but he also seems to associate Aiwass with an entity that is outside of himself. When Crowley makes a statement like "there is no god but man," it seems to indicate that he does not believe in the literal existence of entities, but other of Crowley's writings seem to indicate otherwise. Ultimately, whether Crowley believed in the literal existence of Satan or not is something that students will have to decide for themselves, because Crowley is not here to answer this question for us.

the Snake that giveth Knowledge & Delight and bright glory", and "Think not, o king, upon that lie: That Thou Must Die: verily thou shalt not die, but live." Interestingly, Crowley himself associates Hadit (Aiwass) with Satan.[15]

For centuries, those who have worshipped Satan/Lucifer have seen him as a champion of freedom and individuality, long before the birth of Crowley or LaVey. To give credit to either one of these men for being the originators of the Satanic philosophy would be utterly disrespectful to Satan and his Demons.

THE SATANIC BIBLE

Over the years many Satanists have written to me asking my opinion about *The Satanic Bible. The Satanic Bible* is a great primer for those who are new to Traditional Satanism because it teaches you how to break away from the Judeo-Christian moral codes that so many of us have had programmed into us at a young age. It gives you a philosophy to live by so that you have a foundation on which to base your daily life. It encourages people to live a Satanic lifestyle, which is something that many modern and Traditional Satanists find very hard to do, because we have had all sorts of inaccurate information ingrained in us since birth.

The result is that we have to struggle to think of

---

15 "...The Beast 666 has preferred to let names stand as they are, and to proclaim simply that AIWAZ, the solar-phallic-hermetic 'Lucifer,' is His own Holy Guardian Angel, and 'The Devil' SATAN or HADIT, the supreme soul behind RA-HOOR-KHUIT the Sun.....This serpent, SATAN, is not the enemy of Man, but He who made Gods of our race, knowing Good and Evil......." (Crowley, Magick in Theory and Practice) This is only one example. Others may be found throughout Crowley's writings by the serious student.

things from a truly Satanic perspective rather than a Judeo-Christian one. It is a constant, on-going process that is something that you cannot change overnight. It is something that you will be working on for the rest of your life as a Satanist.

It is not easy to get rid of the guilt that the Christian god and his followers have placed upon us because of their desire to enslave mankind by teaching man that what is natural is wrong. If there is one thing LaVey did very well, it is that he taught people that mankind's natural desires are not evil and that it is perfectly acceptable to indulge in them without guilt. Most importantly, he taught people to think like Satanists and make decisions from a Satanic viewpoint. In the area of morality and escaping Christian programming, *The Satanic Bible* is hands-down one of the best texts a beginning Satanist can read, if you ignore what it says about spirituality.

In the form of Traditional Satanism which I practice, we do not elevate the servant above the Master. We do not raise the messenger to godlike status and give them praise they do not deserve, as many people have done in the cases of Aleister Crowley and Anton LaVey. We see them for what they are, as special people who were chosen by Satan to deliver his message to mankind, and we offer our praise and worship to the one who deserves it, Satan – the one who gave us our freedom and intellect in the first place.

CHAPTER XIII

THE USE OF THE LABEL "REVERSE CHRISTIANITY"

"REVERSE Christianity" is a term that gets thrown around a lot in the Satanic community, especially by modern Satanists. I am not going to debate with you whether this is an accurate description of our religion. This is simply because I know those of you who believe it is an accurate term will continue to believe it is, and those of you who do not will continue to believe it is not.

But what I do want to point out to you is that the people that often use this term like to make the claim they have moved beyond Christianity, much like the neopagans. Yet they spend their time seeking out people whom they believe to be reverse Christians. If Christianity has no relevance if it has no power – if it means nothing – then why do they focus on it? Why do they give it any attention at all? I'll tell you why: because they have not moved beyond it – because they have not learned to leave it behind.

The only reason most of these people that constantly use this term are Satanists at all is because they are rebelling against Christianity. It is the only reason they believe what they believe. If the only reason you call yourself a Satanist or do the rituals you do is because of your hatred of Christianity, you are not much of a Satanist, and what is more reverse Christian than that? You are just a Satanist because you hate Christianity or any faith related to it. Whether it is the Muslim faith, whether it is the Jewish faith, your simple reason for being what you are is an act of rebellion. That is reverse Christianity in my book. If most people took the time to stop and think about what they do and why they do it, they would realize that I am right, and that is exactly what it is.

Most modernists do not practice Satanism because they respect Satan or the old ways, but because they are simply rebelling. As the Church of Satan has said itself, they consider themselves to be "atheists with distinction," and they use the term "Satanism" for shock value and the reaction they get from people. Modern Satanists are very much like atheists in many respects. Just like atheists, modern Satanists will tell you, "Oh, we don't need to talk about god, we don't need to talk about the Devil, they're just superstitions. They mean nothing."

But just like atheists, all they do is talk about Jesus, and whether or not he is the son of the Christian god. All they do is talk about the Christian religion. In fact, they probably spend more time focusing on it, studying it, and giving attention to it than most Christians do!

And that is exactly what people who use the term "reverse Christianity" do: instead of promoting their ideas, instead of promoting their morality, instead of promoting what is important to them, they spend all their time focusing on Christianity or those who believe anything similar to it. It is nothing more than an adult temper tantrum, than somebody going, "I don't believe in Christianity so I'm not going to believe in anything, na na na na!"

They cannot stand that there might be somebody else who's had an experience that they themselves have not had, or has some knowledge of spirituality that they themselves cannot comprehend. So they have to label it as stupid, or superstitious, or ignorant, because they themselves have not had that experience, and therefore, it must not exist. It is a fact that there is a spiritual reality out there, whether they themselves believe it or not, that they have not experienced because Satan or the Demons has probably deemed them unworthy, so they have to accuse everyone else who has had the experience of being a crackpot.

There is a general attitude amongst modern Satanists that they are superior to those of us who worship Satan. But what they do not realize is they have gone against one of the very tenets of *The Satanic Bible* and bought into their own spiritual pipe-dream that they are truly gods.

The evidence that their logic is flawed on this point is shown by the many child custody cases involving Church of Satan members where a mere judge, who is not the highest embodiment of human life, can force them to bend over and take it up the ass without lube. Meanwhile, the Christian woman they are divorcing takes their children away and raises them in the Christian church. If you were a god, you would never allow that to happen, would you?

I do not want anyone reading this to think for a minute that I agree with what has been done to modern Satanists in various court cases. I believe that we as Traditional Satanists should stand with modern Satanists on this issue, because this issue affects us all and it could happen to any Satanist who has children at any time. I am just trying to illustrate how ludicrous it is to have this attitude of superiority compared to those who believe in the literal existence of Satan.

It seems far more unrealistic to think of yourself as

your own god than it does to think that there are spiritual entities out there who influence the evolution of mankind. If you cannot even control a judge in the U.S. Justice System, what kind of god are you? In my opinion, you aren't much of one at all.

Modern Satanists have every right to believe what they want to believe – Satan gave them that freedom, whether they acknowledge him and his gift or not. But for my part, I do not consider them the same religion. I do not consider them from the same family, and I certainly don't think they give Satan and the Demons the respect they deserve. If modern Satanists and the skeptics were truly advocates of free thought as they so often claim to be, then they would mind their own business and leave people with a different religious point of view alone to do their own thing, instead of labeling them "reverse Christians."

CHAPTER XIV

THE IMPORTANCE OF KEEPING A MAGICKAL JOURNAL

ONE of the most important aspects of occult practice that is often overlooked or purposefully shied away from by students is the use of a magickal journal, diary, or Grimoire. By whatever name you call it, this journal is one of the most important things you can do as part of your occult practice, because it gives you an ongoing record of your progress and the spiritual events that are happening around you.

Many occultists would rather have their nails ripped off their fingers than consistently keep a magickal journal, myself included, because they hate the tedium and repetitiveness of documenting every small detail of their spiritual life. Regardless of how annoying it is, it is very important, because it allows you to take a snapshot of what is going on in your life at that moment. It helps you understand how what is going on in your life affects your magickal and spiritual practice. It also allows you to go back and notice recurring themes that you might not have otherwise noticed.

For example, a magickal journal is particularly useful for keeping track of spiritual events such as Demonic communication. Because communication with the Demons can sometimes be very subtle, and can be a mix of symbols and images, rather than words, a magickal journal is particularly useful at detecting these reoccurring events.

Many occultists have different ways of keeping a

magickal journal. Some occultists recommend that you keep a dream journal and a ritual journal. They stress the importance of keeping these two magickal journals separate and distinct from each other. I do not agree. I believe that you should keep a magickal journal but as a combination of a dream journal and a ritual journal, that reads more like a diary. The reason is you can go back at a later date and take out the entries related to rituals and make it a separate journal for magickal invocations, ritual ideas, and the like. And if you feel that a dream is particularly important, you can go back and put it into a separate book.

It is much easier to use one journal to keep up with all your thoughts about magick, occultism, and Satanism than it is to keep up with a separate journal for each thing. Besides, you can easily make up a separate section for each area of interest, as shown on the next page:

MAGICKAL DIARY ENTRY SHEET

Date: Time:

SLEEPING PATTERNS AND DREAM INFO

Time You Went To Sleep: Time You Woke Up:

Additional Notes On Sleeping Patterns:

Dream Entry:

PERSONAL CONDITION

Physical State:

Emotional State:

DIETARY INFORMATION

Breakfast:

Lunch:

Dinner:

Snacks:

Approximate daily Calorie intake:

Dietary Goals and Additional Notes:

Exercise Regiment:

DAILY RITUALS AND MEDITATION

Ritual Type:

Start time:

End Time:

General Notes:

One of the downsides of doing a magickal journal in this format is that it tends to cause a student to use it more as a personal journal rather than a magickal one. You may find yourself going on and on about relationships or personal issues that have absolutely nothing to do with magick. For example, you may create a subsection that is entitled "my emotional state" in order to help you keep an accurate record of your emotions on a day-to-day basis.

In this section you may write down why you're sad, and it may have something to do with your personal relationship with your boyfriend or girlfriend. Because you are so emotional about the situation, it may lead to a 1000-word rant about why your boyfriend or girlfriend is such an ass. It is important to keep a record of why you are in the emotional state that you are in, but the description should only be a line or two, to keep you from getting off-track and making your magickal journal about things other than magickal or spiritual issues. If you want to write about what an asshole your significant other is, that is what personal diaries are for.

You should make every attempt to keep your magickal journal as focused as possible, with only things that are relevant to your daily religious or magickal practices. You should document anything that you feel affects your magickal practice or your spiritual state of being even if it seems insignificant at the time, because you never know how something that seems insignificant may take on greater importance in the future.

For instance, if you notice reoccurring numbers or symbols, you want to document them because it is likely they have some spiritual significance for you. When

Demonic spirits communicate they tend to use pictures, symbols, and numbers to convey messages that can only be understood by the individuals or groups that are observing them. There may be several reasons for this. It could be the individual has not developed themselves psychically or magickally enough that the Demons can communicate with them in any other way except using symbols, numbers, or pictures. Or it might be that the Demon trying to communicate with you might be a lesser spirit who has difficulty manifesting on this plane, or it could be a combination of both.

Many people are unaware of how much energy is required for a spirit to do something that physically manifests on this plane. For example, if a spirit causes a cup to be thrown across the room, that takes a great deal of energy to make that happen, so it is likely that that spirit is far more powerful than his actions might indicate.

Now that we have discussed what should be in a magickal journal, the next obvious question is, "How often should I update my journal?" You should update your magickal journal every day, and if nothing spiritually or magickally significant happened that day, then document that. Do not be too hard on yourself if you forget to update your journal or have a lazy streak. It happens to everyone. If you miss a day, just make a note that this is an entry for the previous day and document anything that was important.

The next question that every student asks after they ask how often they should update their magickal journal is, "What kind of journal should I get?" I feel that the most suitable journal is one where the covers are made of goatskin. It should be consecrated and a protection spell should be placed upon it asking for Satan's blessing upon the student and the magickal or spiritual work that he or she may undertake in Satan's name. If you are unable to find a magickal journal made out of goatskin, any black leather journal will suffice, as long as the proper consecration and blessing has been done.

Because a daily magickal journal is used to keep track of daily events, and it needs to be easy to edit and update, keeping it on a computer is acceptable. Buying a blank journal with any kind of paper and writing your entries with a pen is acceptable. If you want to get more elaborate for your daily magickal journal, that's up to you, but it is unnecessary and impractical for most people.

If you decide to print a hard copy of your magickal journal that you have been keeping on your computer, you should have it bound in a book with goatskin covers or black leather. There are companies that can bind preprinted material in whatever style that suits your taste.

Many people do not understand the difference between a magickal journal and a Grimoire or a Book of Shadows. A magickal journal is a daily record of your personal emotions and magickal and spiritual practices. In short, it is a book that charts your personal development as a Satanist and magician. A personal Grimoire or Book of Shadows is a collection of spells and rituals that you have finalized, and is a ceremonial book used almost exclusively during rituals.

People are often curious about what kind of paper and ink should be used in a personal Grimoire or Book of Shadows. Because a personal Grimoire or Book of Shadows is a collection of personal ceremonies, rituals, invocations, etc., and since it is used almost exclusively during ritual, it should be treated as a magickal object.

And this is the time when you might want to spend the extra money for animal parchment and supplies to make magickal ink. It should also be noted that many groups have a group Grimoire, that is a collection of the group's spells and rituals.

If you're going to spend the extra money to buy animal parchment, you might also want to take a calligraphy class so what you write in your Grimoire will look as elegant as the paper it is written on. Many places do offer calligraphy courses, and also, if you are looking for a recipe for magickal inks, you can find several recipes in Scott Cunningham's *The Complete Book of Incenses, Oils, and Brews*, published in 1989. No matter how you feel about keeping a magickal journal, it is something that every Satanist should strive to do regularly because it can become a very important tool in your spiritual and magickal development.

CHAPTER XV

BOOKS ON SATANISM

DUE to the development of publish-on-demand services such as Lulu, there is more information being published about Satanism every day, giving students access to a variety of different opinions from different theological perspectives. The downside to these services is that there is no quality control; there is no fact checking; there is no confirmation of authors' assertions. As a consequence, anybody who can string more than two words together at a time can publish a book on Satanism, whether they know anything about the religion or not.

Although there is a significant increase in the amount of information published about Satanism, there is still no definitive book on the market that gives accurate information about those of us who worship the Devil. To my knowledge, there are currently no books on the market specifically dedicated to the religious worship of Satan which provide readers with accurate information. In fact, most of the books on Satanism can usually be put into one of four distinct categories:

First are the books written by Christians warning people about the supposed dangers of getting involved in Satanism or the occult. These books are usually written by evangelical preachers who specialize in what is called deliverance ministry, which simply means that they are supposedly experts in dealing with Demonic spirits and Demonic possession. These books are usually marketed to parents who are afraid their children are getting too deeply involved in the occult or Satanism.

These books specialize in scaring parents to death by giving them blow-by-blow accounts of the most horrible murder cases the ministers can find involving teen Satanists. Because the main purpose of these books is to convert people to Christianity, they tend to over exaggerate the frequency of such cases, never really explaining to the reader that while these cases do still occur, they are extremely rare.

They also have a tendency to leave out important facts such as that most of these "Satanic cults" they talk about in their books are not usually connected to any formal Satanic group or any recognized tradition of Satanism. In fact, many of the groups that commonly engage in illegal activity are usually comprised of members new to the Satanic religion, and the majority of their members are under 18 years old.

Another major characteristic of these groups is that the leader of the group is usually no more knowledgeable about Satanism than their followers. Even though teenagers do account for a large percentage of the criminal activity often associated with Satanism, it is still a relatively rare occurrence, which is a fact rarely mentioned by Christian authors when they write about Satanism.

It is even less likely for individuals who have been practicing Satanism for years to be involved in the types of crimes that are described in these books. As they get older and they become more mature Satanists, they quickly begin to realize that engaging in mindless criminal activity does nothing to further our cause. *Satanism: the Seduction of America's Youth* by Bob Larson, published in 1989, is a great example of a book that would fit into this category.

Books like this one, in addition to talk shows such as "Geraldo Rivera," "Sally Jessy Raphael," and "Phil Donahue," which were popular in the mid-80's, helped foster the belief in the criminality of Satanism. The, along with the persistent belief of many Christians that Satanic cults had organized themselves into a nationwide network which engaged in human trafficking, child pornography and prostitution, and human sacrifice led the FBI to publish a report in 1992 that refuted these claims. This hysteria that was perpetuated by many evangelists through pen and pulpit, gave rise to what was eventually termed the "Satanic Panic" of the 80's.

Second are the books written by modern Satanists, like *The Satanic Bible* by Anton LaVey, published in 1969. These are the books that try to convince people that Satan does not really exist. Modern Satanists believe that Satan is just a symbol of the dark forces of nature or the dark side of man. They use Satanism to market their atheistic ideas, and make money to line their own pockets, and they take every opportunity that presents itself to belittle those of us who actually believe in the literal existence of Satan. More often than not, they also help to reinforce the negative assertions the public makes about those of us who worship Satan, such as that we are mentally unstable, or worship Satan simply because we are antisocial individuals that are unable to function in "normal society."

Third are the books that look at Satanism from a purely historical perspective. A good example of books that fit in this category are books that examine how society's views of hell and the Devil have changed through the centuries. *Satanism Today: An Encyclopedia of Religion, Folklore, and Popular Culture* by James R.

Lewis, published in 2001, is an example. Books like these are an excellent source of historical information that help to give us an understanding of our past.

Understanding our past history is a very important aspect of the learning process, because knowing our past prevents us from being misled into believing things that are untrue by those who seek to manipulate those who are naive about the history of our religion. Take for example the Church of Satan, who tries to claim that they created the term Satanism. This statement can be easily refuted by reading the books *A History of Witchcraft and Demonology* by Montague Summers, which was published in 1927, and *The Black Arts* by Richard Cavendish, published in 1967.

Fourth are the books written purely for entertainment value. Stephen King's *Needful Things*, published in 1991, is an excellent example of a book that would fall into this category. Regardless of whether they believe in Satan or not, people are fascinated by him, and as such, he has inspired many artistic endeavors, such as poetry, books, films, paintings, etc.

Man has always been drawn towards things he fears or does not understand, and writers, publishers, and filmmakers have always used people's fascination with the Devil and his minions to make a quick buck. When you have some time, you may want to go to your favorite online bookstore and do a search on Satanism, just to see what comes up. I think you will be just as surprised as I was to find out just how many of the books that come up are written by Christians.

It is downright shocking to consider the amount of money being made off of Satanism by people whose only purpose in life is to undermine the teachings of our religion and slander our god. As much as this bothers me, it does not bother me near as much as the fact that books written by those who seriously worship Satan are virtually nonexistent.

CHAPTER XVI

DAILY PRAYER

IN this chapter we are going to talk about one of the most important aspects of a Devil Worshiper's religious life: daily prayer. Without a strong connection to Satan, everything else that you do is really irrelevant. Prayer is one of the most simple, effective ways to make a connection with Satan and his Demons. By doing daily prayer ritual, you get connected to the spirits you worship.

There is a presence that you feel when you have successfully done a prayer ritual. Many people are surprised, even shocked, at how peaceful and centered they feel when they do a prayer ritual, because whether we realize it or not many of us have bought into this Christian idea that Satan is the personification of evil, that he is only negative, albeit only subconsciously. When they feel this connection with Satan, it is completely unexpected. But that does happen if you do your prayer rituals on a regular basis and you do them with a sincere heart.

Donald Michael Craig, in his book *Modern Magick: Eleven Lessons in the High Magickal Arts*, says that he believes about 99% of the people that talk about the occult and magick do not actually practice, and I would say the same is true of those who worship Satan. It is only a small percentage of people who actually practice this religion, and that is something that I want to change, and I hope I can do that through this book.

Don't be the type of person who boasts about how

they practice rituals, and worship Satan, and then sit on your ass with a bag of potato chips in front of the TV all day. It makes you a hypocrite, and there is nothing worse than that. If you wanted to be a hypocrite, you might as well have been a Christian. You don't have to be a Satanist. Christians are the ultimate hypocrites. If you say you worship Satan, you say you practice rituals, then do it.

People write to me asking me what they should do. My suggestion is that you do a simple prayer ritual, approximately 5-7 minutes in length. You do a scripted opening, a scripted closing, and an unscripted middle section where you speak from the heart and talk to Satan the way you would to a friend or parent. Scripting the opening is very important because it helps you get out of the everyday mindset and gets you into a more spiritual frame of mind.

The opening, meaning the purification, has very little spiritual significance aside from the fact that you purify the area before you get started. The opening and closing are there to impose structure and order into the ritual. What is important to the spirits is that you come to them with sincerity and talk to them the way you would talk to a friend or family member.

Remember, these are your gods that you are talking to, the entities that you want to spend eternity with, and if you cannot even talk to them without giving a prepared speech, what kind of relationship can you expect to have? Also, it can get boring for the spirits, as well as yourself, after you say the same things over and over again.

When you have been doing these rituals for six months or more, you will probably start to get bored, and you will start to do your rituals and invocations in a very listless way. So if you start feeling that your primary invocation or your ritual is getting stale, or that it is losing its meaning or that you are not connecting the way that you should be, change it up. Add something to it, take something away, whatever you have to do.

As you are doing these rituals, there will be some days when you do not think you have done a very good job and you may feel that you have let the spirits down. Just come at it the next day and do it again. If you worry about every ritual being perfect and you are hard on yourself because you are worried that you did not perform it correctly, you will never truly let go and achieve a spiritual connection with Satan or the Demons. If your mind is consumed with guilt over the mistakes you have made, it cannot focus on experiencing the relationship. So if you do not do something right, just forget about it, and try to improve on it the next day.

Now let us move on to a discussion of the invocation. There are a few points you should keep in mind: your invocation should be something simple and mantra-like. It is incredibly helpful if the invocation is short, rhythmic, and rhymes.

When you first enter your ritual area, you want to take some time out before you even start your ritual to do some basic breathing and relaxation techniques in order to tell your subconscious mind that you are no longer concerned with the mundane aspects of life. This is an especially important step for me personally, because if something is bothering me, I focus on it. If I am having personal problems in a relationship, or with a family member, it will distract me from my rituals.

One of the things that work for me is to come up with an image that can go along with the invocation. For example, "Satan, I invoke thee" while visualizing Satan possessing me and speaking through me as I am doing that part of the invocation, and as I am visualizing that, it keeps my mind focused and does not allow me to be distracted by other thoughts. It is a type of meditation, although some would argue that it does not fit the technical definition of a full meditative experience. But it is useful for keeping your mind focused on what you are doing.

As you are doing your ritual, come up with images that you feel you connect with. For example, if you are addressing Lucifer, then have an image of Lucifer in your mind. If you are doing an invocation to Satan, do the same thing, and this will keep you from having mundane thoughts coming into your mind and disrupting your ritual. Now, even when you do this you will still have some difficulty, but it will help a great deal.

The main thing is to be a practicing Satanist instead of one of those people who claim to worship Satan. If you are going to say you are a practicing Satanist, be one. Have enough respect for Satan and yourself to practice what you preach. By doing this, you will be an example for others. Besides, Satanism has enough hypocrites already – it doesn’t need any more. Once you start doing daily prayer, you will wonder how you did without it.

I want to continue discussing visualization. For some, visualizing these elaborate images of Lucifer or Satan may be difficult at first. One of the things I found to be most effective is to visualize the name Satan or Lucifer in my mind when I was having difficulty focusing. If I would lose that thought, I would just focus on something else related to Satan or Lucifer until I could bring my mind back to what I was originally visualizing.

Another thing you want to remember is if you lose a thought, that's okay. If your mind drifts off and starts thinking about mundane things, just redirect it to focusing on the ritual, the visualization, or the words you are saying. For many people, it takes quite a while to get focused on what you are doing, and the reason I give these techniques is if you do not find some way to keep your mind focused, the regular things of everyday life will intrude.

This is supposed to be your time with Satan and the Demons, so you want to do your best, although you are not going to be perfect, and the Demons understand that. As long as you put your best effort forward and are well intentioned, they will appreciate what you have done for them.

Here are a few other suggestions for when you are distracted and you do not feel you are mentally prepared to begin your ritual. When you are not focused, light your candles, ring your bell to consecrate your room, and say your consecration. Once you have finished the consecration portion of the ritual, sit down, be as still as possible, inhale and exhale slowly, and relax. Do this as long as it takes to get you into a calm state of mind. Do not put any time limit on it. Do not rush through this step in the process. Spend time thinking about Satan and the ritual you are about to do.

The ritual should be short enough that it is something you can do in the morning before you go to work and in the evening before you go to bed. You should never do your ritual when you are in a rush. There are going to be times when it is unavoidable and it is going to happen, but you should always give yourself sufficient time to do your rituals appropriately and with respect.

Many books say that you should do your rituals at the same time every day so that your mind is programmed to know that it is time for ritual, but I disagree. You will naturally find the time that works best for you. When I started doing daily rituals, I found that what worked best was doing what came natural to me. When I tried to impose a schedule on myself, I found it very difficult to keep, and it discouraged me and made me less enthusiastic about doing daily rituals.

I typically do my daytime ritual between 10:30 and 11:30 in the morning, and my evening rituals between 10:30 or 11:30 at night. If you just do it when it feels most natural, you will find that you are keeping a fairly regular schedule without even trying. I recommend that you do both a morning ritual and an evening ritual, so that you have at least two times a day that you focus on Satan. The morning ritual should be focused on Lucifer, and the evening ritual should be focused on Satan. If you wish, you could also add a third prayer that focuses on Baphomet as the unification of both aspects. If you do that you will find that you feel more centered and connected.

Do not wait too late to do your evening rituals, because when you start to repeat your invocation, especially if it is written in a mantra-type style, it is likely to have an almost hypnotic effect which is likely to put you to sleep if you are extremely tired. If you are tired, it is better to do your ritual early than to wait and do it at your usual time. It is better to do it early and do a shorter ritual than it is to do your standard ritual, and end up falling asleep or end up doing a half-assed job. All the things that I have brought up thus far may seem like common sense to experienced practitioners, but this section is not being written with you in mind. This section is being written for the inexperienced.

Many people do not discuss the practical issues that a practitioner may face because they do not practice. There are many people who write books that will give you all kinds of advice, even though they themselves do not actually practice. I read a book by Donald Tyson called *New Millennium Magic* where he says that there are authors who write for his publishing company who do not even practice the things they write about.

These things I am imparting to you are things I have learned through actual experience, and unlike authors who write for major publishing companies, none of the money I make off this book is for personal use. All the money made from this book goes directly toward promoting Satanism. I want to see people actually practice and preserve the Satanic religion. You should never take anybody's word, especially when it comes to occultism. If you follow my advice, the results should speak for themselves. If you try anything in this book, I would like to hear from you, because I always like to hear about people's experiences.

If you see an invocation in a book that really touches you, use it. If a piece of someone else's ritual inspires you – for example, three or four lines in an invocation – then use them and omit the rest. I am not one who believes you should not mix and match rituals. I do not believe anything detrimental will happen to you by doing this. I have never had a negative experience myself, and I believe that you should use parts of rituals that touch you and draw some emotion out of you, so that you can begin to build a relationship with Satan and the Demons.

Whether it is a ritual or an invocation from antiquity

or modern times, so be it – whatever works for you. If you want to add some original content to the ritual, then that is what you should do. However, I believe there is one exception to this: rituals that have an ancient tradition or have a long history, for example, Black Sabbaths, should not be altered from their original form. By altering them, they will lose some of their potency, and it is the very history of these rituals that gives them some of their power.

Writing an original ritual that is suited to your personal taste is the best way to go, in my opinion, because a ritual that evokes genuine emotion and comes from the heart is far more effective than a ritual that is being performed by rote. Many inexperienced practitioners do not understand that it is not the objects used in a ritual or the sigils that are magickal, but it is the emotion with which they are made. Every part of a ritual, whether it is the invocation or the magickal items that are used during the ritual, are empowered by the emotion of the practitioner, and the relationship they have with their god. Spirits have emotions and they are drawn to expressions of emotion.

To illustrate the importance that strong emotions play in rituals, let me give you the following example: I did an experiment once just to see if it would work. I focused on a candle and asked the Demonic spirits to send a message to a girlfriend of mine and give her the desire to call me. She had not called me in several weeks, but with all my anger focused on the candle flame I said, "Send this message through this candle flame, carry it to her, spirits both named and nameless," and she called me the very next day. She called me and told me I had been on her mind a lot and she felt the desire to call me.

This is an excellent example of how strong emotion combined with a genuine belief in the Demonic spirits can achieve results. As you can see, I did not do an elaborate ritual. I just used an ordinary black candle, focused my emotions on it, and asked the Demonic spirits to deliver a message on my behalf. The only thing I did prior to doing this was a basic consecration of the room in order to prepare for ritual, using incense and ringing the bell as described above. So it is not so much what you do, it is how you do it.

CHAPTER XVII

MARRIAGE, SEX, AND RELATIONSHIPS

IN my approach, I believe it is a mistake for a Traditional Satanist (Devil Worshiper) to get involved in a romantic relationship with someone who is not also a Traditional Satanist. This is because if you are a dedicated Satanist, why would you want to be with someone who is without? Why would they even interest you? The mere fact that you are with someone who is without would cause most dedicated, diehard Satanists to question your dedication.

For me personally, I have no interest in being in a romantic relationship with someone who is not a Satanist. In fact, the thought of being in a romantic relationship with somebody who is not a Satanist totally disgusts me. The reason it disgusts me is because I do not want to be emotionally attached to someone who is dirt. It would be like a rancher falling in love with his livestock. A cow is there to be eaten or used for survival. It is not there to be romanced.

Being in a relationship with someone who is without is essentially, in our view, cross-species mating because we believe that Satanists are a race unto themselves, and are spiritually different in their very essence from those who are without. Being in a relationship with someone who is without can have potentially negative effects on a Satanist's spiritual life.

First, I have found that Satanists who are involved in a relationship with non-Satanists usually have a relationship that goes very well for a while, but eventually, the differences in religious opinion and morality usually start to surface impact the stability of the relationship. And in situations like this, something has to give: either one's religious devotion, or the relationship. Eventually, the partner who is a Satanist, if they are serious about their Satanism, will be faced with having to make the decision about what is more important to them – their religion, or their relationship.

Second, if a Satanist is in a relationship with someone who is without, they are probably not dedicating themselves to Satan the way they should because they are dividing their time between Satan and the person who is without. If you are in a relationship with someone who is a Satanist, they are not going to be resentful of the time you spend with Satan, or the religious obligations that you make to him, because they themselves are probably doing the very same things.

When a Satanist is confronted with this kind of decision it can be highly emotional and weigh very heavily on them. Even if they are a devoted Satanist and would never choose their personal relationship over Satan, they have still grown very emotionally attached to the person they are with, and may find it extremely difficult to sever that relationship.

If you add children into the mix, you can see how this would make things a hundred times worse. Not only do you have to deal with the emotions that you and your partner are feeling, but you have to deal with how the children are feeling, so it is best to avoid the whole nasty business altogether by not putting yourself in this type of situation.

SATANIC SEX

Any type of sexual intercourse or sexual play between consenting adults is acceptable, so long as the people involved in it are not doing it against their will. No Satanist should allow themselves to be coerced or manipulated into doing something they do not want to, because that is un-Satanic.

You should always go into everything you do by choice, even if that is giving up your free will for a set period of time, as in the case of a submissive to a dominant, or a slave to master (in a BDSM relationship). An individual can submit to another and give up their will to another by choice, for any length of time they so desire.

This idea of someone giving up their free will willingly, without being coerced, is sometimes hard for some to understand, but there are individuals out there who truly have a desire to be a servant or a slave to others. While these individuals are rare, especially among Satanists, the fact remains that they do exist, and as Satanists, we accept people of all sexual orientations and lifestyles, because Satan does not judge.

I need to take a moment here to mention an important distinction between sexual relationships and marriage. While I do advocate very strict rules about marrying outside the religion, these same rules do not apply when concerning the selection of a sexual partner. I believe that Satanists can have sex with whoever they choose, whether they are a Satanist or not.

The only condition is that Satanists should never get a non-Satanist pregnant, or be impregnated by a non-Satanist. It is okay to select a partner for sexual gratification who is not a Satanist, but it is not okay to marry or procreate with a non-Satanist. I personally frown on procreating outside of the religion, simply because I believe that Satan would rather His children be with each other, than be with someone who is without.

SATANIC MARRIAGE

Many people have different ideas about what Satanic marriage is. In my approach, marriage is seen as a method by which we as Satanists preserve the Satanic tradition and the Satanic bloodline, or "race." We believe that Satanists should not marry outside the religion, because it dilutes the blood and it dilutes the spiritual essence that is strengthened by the unification of two individuals who have dedicated themselves mind, body, and soul to the Lord of Darkness.

When someone dedicates themselves to Satan, they are changed spiritually, and that spiritual change can be carried through the DNA to their children. Local Covens should encourage marriage amongst their members not only because of the potential for the strengthening of the genes that will be passed along to their children, but also for the social stability that marriage provides. It is much easier to walk away from your responsibilities, including your children, when you are unmarried. If you have a legal commitment to your partner, it is much more difficult to walk away when things in a relationship are not going the way we think they should.

The fact that I encourage my readers to get married should not be seen as an issue of morality, it should be seen as an issue of survival. As with all the teachings presented in this volume, everything that I preach is with an emphasis on trying to help build a strong, stable Satanic community, and I see marriage as the most efficient way to create and maintain that stability.

ACCEPTABLE FORMS OF MARRIAGE IN SATANISM

In Traditional Satanism or Devil Worship, the individuals involved in a relationship are free to decide what type of marriage suits them best, because Satan gives us that freedom.[16] Hence, it would be inappropriate for us to have any other point of view than to say that any form of marriage that is agreed to by two or more parties involved is acceptable. Heterosexual, same-sex, polygamous, or open marriages would be acceptable among Traditional Satanists.

However, because of the predominant influence of the Abrahamic religious traditions, society has deemed polygamous and homosexual marriage to be illegal. Because our society is based on a Christian moral code, it is directly at odds with Satanism and our beliefs, and because we refuse to capitulate to Christian morality, we recognize polygamy and homosexual marriage as a legitimate form of marriage.

A proper Coven is run based on Satan's morality, not the Christian god's. "*Who desireth me must forsake the world.*" (From "The Poem in Praise of Sheikh Adi"; See Appendix.) As long as the individuals who are involved in the relationship have set ground rules and have agreed upon them, then it is okay in Satan's eyes.

16 I allow everyone to follow the dictates of his own nature, but he that opposes me will regret it sorely. (*Al-Jilwah*)

CHAPTER XVIII

ANIMAL SACRIFICE

OF all the subjects discussed in this book, there is none more controversial and more hotly debated than the subject of animal sacrifice. Those who oppose animal sacrifice say it is a cruel and outdated practice that is unnecessary in our day and age. There are several reasons why I believe people hold these beliefs and I will be discussing each one of them in due course. But the main reason I believe people hold these beliefs is due to something that is rather ever discussed either because people have been to afraid to say it or people haven't thought about the subject deeply enough to come to this conclusion for themselves.

And the reason is that most of us no matter how much we talk about our religion or how much we say we believe in our religion really don't believe in the gods and goddesses we worship. If we did, if we genuinely believed in them, than surely, giving a life to them to sustain them or honor them would not be too much to ask because after all, most of us don't have a problem with killing another animal or taking a life if it benefits us. But the same people have a problem with the idea of sacrificing a life to a being that is far more knowledgeable and superior to them. Even though in most religions it is believed that that being or those beings created the very life that we're offering back to them so in essence, that god or goddess created that life.

So why would it be a sin to sacrifice that life back to the one who created it? The only conclusion I can come to that logically answers this question for me is just maybe, despite how religious some people appear to be, they really don't believe in their gods and goddesses in a literal sense. Maybe for some people it is exactly like the atheists and modern Satanists have always suggested. They have created a god in their own image, a god in their own minds that shares their beliefs, their morality, and their agenda, rather than actually worshipping a god that literally exists outside of themselves.

The best evidence to support the idea that there are some among us who tend to shape the gods and goddesses in their own image can be found in those who oppose animal sacrifice. They oppose animal sacrifice despite the fact that almost every culture and almost every religion has practiced animal sacrifice since the beginning of time. If the gods are eternal and beyond time and space what has happened to make it to where animal sacrifice was acceptable back then but not acceptable now? Those who oppose animal sacrifice and claim to believe in the gods and goddesses, demons or demonesses never seem to have a logical answer for this question.

I would argue that the gods and goddesses have not changed, and it is man and his morality that has changed and that if it was acceptable to offer them animal sacrifices back then it is still acceptable today. I would even take it a step further and not only suggest to you that they are not worshiping the gods or goddesses as they are, but they've done nothing more than created an elaborate servitor or familiar and named it the god or goddess they claim to believe in.

Because if they were actually worshiping the god or goddess they claim to worship, they would honor the traditions and rituals of that god or goddess as closely as they can, rather than changing it to for what they believe is socially acceptable. If the god or goddess is eternal and is beyond time and space then it is logical to assume that what they requested of their followers has not changed in that time. It is a foolish notion to believe that just because society has changed, just because society has said that these things are not socially acceptable, that the god or goddess you claim to worship necessarily agrees with that belief.

Apart from the previous reasons I just mentioned, there are several factors that contribute to most people's deeply held beliefs about animal sacrifice whether they realize it or not. Not the least of which is the fact that many of us have grown up in cities and lost our touch with nature. If you grow up in a rural environment you have more of a practical understanding of the natural cycles of life and more of a connection with nature just by the fact that you are probably exposed to livestock. And if you are exposed to livestock even in just a passing way you have a tendency to see more of the natural state of things in the sense that you see animals being born, going through different stages of life and you inevitably see animals die. Additionally, if you are a hunter you have more of an understanding of the predator/prey mentality and the natural instincts of animals, whereas people who have grown up in the city have no connection whatsoever with that idea. A hunter understands that everything lives and everything dies and most of the animals that we use in animal sacrifice are essentially prey animals.

If the animals commonly used in Satanic ritual weren't being raised in a pet store and if they weren't being taken care of by the people who are sacrificing them, they would have already been inevitably eaten by a predator and had a very short life span anyway. This is a fact that very few people who are opposed to animal sacrifice ever really consider. Many of the animals used in animal sacrifice have had a better and longer life than they would have had if left in their natural environment. As I said before, many of these animals such as rabbits or rats or whatever it is people may use are generally prey animals and are killed in mass quantities by predators as a natural consequence of living their lives in the wild anyway.

Another factor that many animal rights activists don't want to talk about is the fact that if these prey animals were in the wild, the cruelty and brutality they would suffer at the hands of another animal is far worse than anything that would be done in a Satanic ritual. If you try to explain this to someone who is opposed to animal sacrifice they will inevitably come back with such an argument as "Yeah, but the animal that killed that other animal was doing it to survive, not merely as an act of religious worship." This is simply not true.

Many animals will kill another animal simply because they are bored or they want something to do or another animal was invading their territory, not because they did it to survive or for food, but just because they wanted to. If you watch any program about animals on television that accurately documents animal behavior you will see time and time again where animals kill just for the sake of killing. So to have this idealized point of view about nature or animal behavior that is so prevalent in our society really does you no service.

If you are considering whether or not to add animal sacrifice to your religious practices you should take the time to look at it from a non biased point of view and really try to understand the natural world and animal behavior for what it really is. Many of our views on animals especially now in this society are based on the images and the ideas that have been forced fed upon us by animal rights activists. Now I'm not trying to say that animals are not thinking intelligent beings with feelings. But what I am trying to suggest to you is this notion that they're all peace, love, light, and harmony with the universe is a concept that is contrary to the actual reality of nature itself. Again I want to emphasize that the things animals do to each other in the natural course of survival in the wild is far crueler than anything we would do to them as part of our religious practices.

We have lost our connection with nature and we no longer have to hunt and gather our own food, therefore we no longer see ourselves as the apex predators we are and were meant to be. The idea for taking a life either for food or for sacrifice is considered by many to be barbaric. It should also be noted that because of our affluence and because we don't have to hunt for our food we have begun to humanize animals and see them as members of the family rather than prey or a lesser species. That is why so many people have a problem with the idea of animal sacrifice.

Because things in our society are so convenient and readily available and your hamburger comes in a nice wrapper, people really don't think about what it takes to bring that animal to your dinner table. As a matter of fact some people seem to almost subconsciously disconnect the fact that their hamburger or that piece of chicken was an animal at all. Logically they know where the meat comes from, but they've become so disassociated with the more gruesome aspects of animal slaughter that they don't even consciously think of it as an animal anymore because they so used to seeing it in a plastic wrapper. So when they're confronted with someone who has a religious practice that actually takes a living animal and slaughters it for their god, this invisible being that they cant see or hear, they think its totally useless or barbaric.

But I would hope that because Satanism is supposed to be a religion of the flesh as well as the spirit, the animal as well as the spiritual, Satanists would not be so quick to jump on the anti-sacrifice bandwagon. Especially those people who are traditional Devil Worshipers who want to revise the old ways. I hope that by the time you're through with this chapter I will have made strong enough arguments and given you enough info so that you can make an informed decision about whether animal sacrifice is right for you as a part of your religious practices. Far too many people automatically jump to a socially acceptable conclusion on this issue based on an emotional knee jerk reaction.

Now that we've discussed many of the reasons why those who opposes animal sacrifice have issues with it lets move on to explain why Satanists like me practice animal sacrifice. First, we do not practice animal sacrifice because we are a bunch of teenagers who get some kind of sick thrill out of inflicting unnecessary pain on another living creatures.

In my approach, offering an animal to Satan or the Demons is a sign of respect. We are sacrificing a life to them and because it is a life it has value. But beyond that, we are offering the spirits sustenance because we believe that when the spirits are present they feed off the energy or life force of the animal in question. I believe that it takes a great deal of energy for the spirits to interact with our world. This holds true whether they interact in the sense that they come to witness a ritual that is being held for them or when they intercede on our behalf to help changes occur in our world in accordance with the practitioner's will.

That is one of the key differences in my religious beliefs and magickal system. My magickal system is not based on the idea that the power to change the universe in accordance with ones will simply comes from the individual or the power of the individual soul. It is based on the belief that things that occur in this world are directly related to how the spirits interact with this world. In other words the spirits who we call upon are not merely spectators that watch things happen to mankind. They directly interact with mankind and influence events and circumstances to happen in a way so that their worshipers will meet the destiny that they were born for. Since we believe that things can change based on the opinion or decisions of Satan and his demons it only seems logical that we would try to do things to show respect and reverence for them, especially if we wanted them to intercede on our behalf in a particular situation.

I'm not suggesting that a Demon's personal intercession on your behalf is the main reason that you should sacrifice. In my view the best sacrifice and the most respectful sacrifice is the one that you do without asking for anything in return. There is another philosophical point that I am trying to convey by attempting to revive the practice of animal sacrifice within the context of a Satanic tradition. And this point is that nothing is free. Everything has a price, even in Satan's Kingdom. And it is the height of rudeness to come to Satan's altar and ask for his assistance and do nothing for Him or His kingdom in return.

You see, in Western cultures in particular we have become very self oriented and many people feel entitled to have anything and everything they want without having to work for it or pay a price. I believe this is because for many people religion has become nothing more than an adult security blanket. They say they believe in their gods because it makes them feel secure or important. But in many peoples cases I really don't think they believe at all because if they truly believed in the literal existence of their deity, making an offering to them such as an animal life or other object wouldn't be that big of a deal.

In rural non-Western cultures the fact that they believe in their gods in a literal sense is very apparent because they offer the best of what they have whether its their animals, their precious metals, or their food, they offer some of it to their gods. In many cases they give the gods the first choice: the best cuts of meats, the best animal, the best and most expensive objects. It is clear that they truly believe in the spirits they worship as literal entities because they give some of everything they have and more often than not, as I have said, they give their gods and goddesses first choice. The fact that there are so many people in our religion that are reluctant to do the same is to me an indication of how little we actually do believe in Satan and the Demons.

Before I go any further I would like to make a very important point. Many modern occultists would argue that animal sacrifice is unnecessary in terms of raising energy for a magickal purpose. Once again I would like to state for the record that the primary purpose of animal sacrifice in our particular tradition is not to raise energy for a magickal purpose but rather to pay homage to the entities we worship. That is not to say that we never use animal sacrifice as a way to raise magickal energy. It is just not the primary reason why we do it.

The argument that those who are opposed to using animal sacrifice as part of a magickal ritual like to use is that there is more energy in a single orgasm than there is in the life and death struggle of an animal to survive, and my response is "Nonsense." I refuse to believe that there is more energy produced by an orgasm during sexual intercourse than there is in the life and death struggle for a living creature to survive. Not only is the idea of an orgasm being more intense than an animal's struggle to survive laughable, but there are far more learned magicians than I that believe animal sacrifice had its place in ritual. Aleister Crowley was one of them. Aleister Crowley not only performed animal sacrifice but he also combined it with sexual ritual in order to raise magickal energy. The idea of combining sacrifice and sexual rituals to raise magickal energy is not exclusive to Aleister Crowley. There have been other accounts that indicate sacrifice and sex are used in the same ritual to raise magickal or spiritual energy.

I'm still shocked at how simple-minded people are when it comes to animal sacrifice. They either think that it is done to raise magickal energy to achieve a specific result in a spell or they think that it is a way to pay homage to one's god. Neither one of these ideas are wrong, but it amazes me that out of the two, people are more likely to think of it in the terms of the former. This is clear evidence at least to me anyway, that very few people actually respect the idea of religious worship and religious observances. They automatically jump to the conclusion that it must be for some selfish purpose, that there can be no desire on the part of the practitioner just to make an offering out of respect for one's gods. Not only does it shock me that people think this way but it also indicates to me that they are not very knowledgeable about religion or magick. Because for people to have such a knee jerk reaction and such a fundamental lack of understanding of how sacrifice is important in magickal and religious ritual is just an indication of how ignorant they really are, both spiritually and magickally.

Now that I've explained why we do animal sacrifice the next obvious question becomes what to sacrifice. This is really a matter of personal choice. Traditionally some Grimoires say that a white mouse was sacrificed to Lucifer. In our tradition any type of animal is an acceptable sacrifice with the exception of black cats and goats. When you pick an animal to sacrifice to Lucifer the animal should be pure white with the exception of its feet and, in the case of rats, its tail.

The reason white animals are selected as an offering to Lucifer is because the white animal is symbolic of the lighter aspect of Satan's nature. It is also a symbol of the fact that Lucifer is a solar deity. Also it could be argued that it denotes the heavenly origins of Lucifer himself as a fallen angel because if you look at Greek tradition white animals were sacrificed to those who were thought to reside in the heavenly realm or mount Olympus and black animals were sacrificed to the spirits of the underworld. So in a sense, by the fact that our tradition and many traditions sacrifice white animals to Lucifer it could almost been seen as symbolically representing that he was once a spirit that inhabited the heavenly realms.

If you have never performed an animal sacrifice there are a couple of things to keep in mind. Number one the actual process of finding the animal is part of the religious devotion. That is why you should go out of your way to find the most perfect animal you can find. When you are looking for an animal, whether it is a pure black animal for Satan or pure white for Lucifer, you should go out of your way to find an animal that is perfect, that has no discoloration at all on any part of its body. You'd be surprised at how many people who perform animal sacrifice will go some where and grab the first animal they can find that kind of fits the requirement, and that's not what were trying to do here.

You want an animal that is healthy, active, that has been well fed, well cared for, and fits the requirements as closely as possible. If that means you have to drive twenty miles out of your way and pay a bit extra to get the best animal possible then that's what you should do. The idea behind an animal sacrifice is it's a way of showing love and respect for your god and not only does selecting poor sacrifices disrespect Satan or Lucifer, it devalues the life of the animal. You're not even sacrificing the animal with enthusiasm and saying, "You are an excellent example of your species you're a beautiful animal that is worthy of being sacrificed to my god." Instead, what you're saying is "Eh, you'll do." Throw it in the box and carry it home. That's not the idea behind giving an offering. The idea behind giving an offering is to pick the best animal you can find, the most beautiful, healthy animal you can find, or even the nicest, most pleasant animal you can find, and take care of that animal to the best of your ability until its sacrificed. That includes playing with the animal, spending time with the animal, and developing a connection with the animal.

What makes it a sacrifice is the fact that it means something to you. If you just kind of go out there and take it willy nilly, you shove it in a box and don't even look at the animal until the time you sacrifice it, then really you're not showing proper respect for the animal or for Satan. It's important to take time to get to know that animal so that you have a connection with it, so that it has some value to you and so that its life means something to both you and Satan. If you totally ignore the animal up until the time you sacrifice it then it really doesn't have any value to you. It's absolutely meaningless.

It should be obvious to anyone reading this chapter that the popular notion of Satanists who sacrifice pets stolen from other people's backyards as an offering to Satan is absolutely ridiculous. One of the important aspects of sacrifice is that you go out of your way to look for and pay for it. It is an offering that comes from your heart and its something that you either have raised yourself or purchased with your own money. That's part of the process. So to steal someone else's animal would not be a true sacrifice because as I have said previously if the animal has no value to you personally and all you did was go grab the first thing you could catch then it has no value as a sacrifice. The idea of a sacrifice is that the item or animal has a personal value and importance to you and obviously if you raised it or paid for it, it would have a personal value to you, but if you stole it, it surely would not.

Some of you may be wondering why I even bother bringing up this subject of theft and why I even bother discussing it in this chapter. The reason is, believe it or not, there are many people who still believe what they see in the movies there are still people who believe everything the media tells them and believe every urban legend they've ever heard. As a Satanist you have to take every opportunity to correct people's misconceptions about your religion because they're getting so much info from so many different sources that have very little first hand knowledge of what Satanism is actually about. You have to constantly stress that your religion is not how the media portrays it to be.

If you are a novice when it comes to animal sacrifice you really should start out with some of the smallest animals possible because this first sacrifice is going to be a very emotional experience no matter what size the animal is. A lot of people find that even if they're experienced hunters and have grown up hunting all their life, the first experience of sacrificing an animal with your own two hands on an altar dedicated to Satan is a very different experience than hunting or butchering an animal in the context of preparing it for food. The second reason for picking a small animal is because when an animal is dying it will do everything it can to fight for its life.

Many people are overwhelmed by the strength of even the smallest animal when its fighting to survive, not to mention the fact that you will probably be extremely nervous if it's the first time you've sacrificed and you're likely to be shaky and unstable yourself. So you don't want to pick an animal that has the capability of hurting you or any people who might be attending the sacrifice too severely. Also, just because an animal is small does not mean you should underestimate the damage that they are capable of doing. In fact, hamsters, gerbils, and rats all have razor sharp teeth that are more than capable of biting down to the bone. The reason I suggest smaller animals is that as long as you maintain control over the position of the animal's head you should be able to sacrifice the animal with relatively little danger to yourself or other participants in the ritual.

Another thing you want to keep in mind as you prepare to do your sacrifices is you want to make sure that you have a knife sharp enough to do the job. No matter how sharp the knife that you have is, there is a strong possibility that it might not be sharp enough to do the job. Animal hide is incredibly tough and even some of the sharpest common knives have difficulty cutting through animal hide and fur. So whatever knife you might have you either want to sharpen it more, or, you might even want to consider getting a knife manufactured for the cutting of animal hide, and using it specifically for the purpose of sacrifice. This is what I recommend because animal sacrifice is supposed to be a magickal act and you really shouldn't be a using a kitchen knife or something else that's lying around the house anyway.

What I recommend is a titanium blade knife, either a hunting knife or a military grade knife. Titanium blades can be sharpened to the point where it rivals the sharpness of a scalpel and that's actually what you really need because that will ensure that you kill the animal as quickly as possible, which is easier for you and more humane for the animal. Besides, a quick death with a minimum of or no pain to the animal is the only legal way to sacrifice animals for religious purposes. Especially if this is your fist sacrifice you really want do want try to make it as easy a process as possible because the first one you do is going to be the most emotional and the most traumatic for you personally and that is true for most people. Of course there will always be people for whom it is no big deal, however.

The one thing you want to keep in mind is that this is supposed to be an offering to your god, a religious ritual and the sacrifice should be conducted with a degree of seriousness and decorum that is appropriate for religious ritual. By performing animal sacrifice you are carrying on a tradition that goes back hundreds and thousands of years. I'm sad to say unfortunately that there are those who approach animal sacrifice as some kind of novelty, something they do to get their thrills, their kicks, living out their Jeffrey Dahmer-like serial killer fantasy of mutilating animals and trying to prove how tough they are.

It's usually the people of this mentality that are most responsible for giving Satanists a bad reputation and creating the negative stereotypes often associated with Satanism. When people find animals disemboweled in their yard and people haphazardly put "Satanic" symbols around it to make it appear as part of a "Satanic" ritual, this is usually what is motivating these people. Aside from the fact that they're trying to play a prank on someone, they're usually people who are sadistic individuals who have the desire to kill and torture animals and they'll use almost any excuse to do it.

Once a sacrifice is done the animal's body should be left upon the altar for at least 24 hours to allow the gods to partake of whatever spiritual essence they wish and then the animal should be consumed by flame. If it is absolutely impossible for the animal to be burned you can bury it, but this should only be done if there truly is no way to build a fire and burn the animal. Traditionally animals offered to infernal spirits or spirits of the underworld were burned.

APPENDIX

HOLY TEXTS OF THE YEZIDIS WITH A COMMENTARY ON THE *AL-JILWAH*

CONSIDERED one of the most sacred texts in the Satanic religion my many practitioners, including myself, the first of the two works included in this appendix is the *Al-Jilwah*. It is traditionally believed to be the direct word of Satan as spoken to His people. The *Al-Jilwah* is a sacred text in the Yezidi religion, a near ancient form of Devil Worship. The Yezidis are a tribe of Kurdish-speaking people concentrated in Northern Iraq. It is said by these people that their religion goes back more than 6,000 years, making it possibly one of the oldest extant religions in the world. Sheikh Adi, their one time leader and chief saint, is said to have received the *Al-Jilwah*, or *Book of Revelation*, in the 12th century A.D. shortly before his death. Also included in this appendix is my commentary on the *Al-Jilwah*. These are my personal opinions and should not be taken as doctrine. They are only being included here to give the student insight that they might otherwise overlook. The second Yezidi text in this Appendix is "The Poem in Praise to Sheikh Adi." It is also attributed to Sheikh Adi. It is said to have been written around the same time that Adi committed the *Al-Jilwah* to writing. It is not as widely used in Satanism as the *Al-Jilwah*, but I personally feel a Satanic presence in this text and include it here for further guidance and inspiration to the student.

AL- JILWAH
THE REVELATION

BEFORE all creation this revelation was with Melek Tâ'ûs, who sent 'Abd Tâ'ûs to this world that he might separate truth known to his particular people. This was done, first of all, by means of oral tradition, and afterward by means of this book, *Al-Jilwah*, which the outsiders may neither read nor behold.

CHAPTER I

I was, am now, and shall have no end. I exercise dominion over all creatures and over the affairs of all who are under the protection of my image. I am ever present to help all who trust in me and call upon me in time of need. There is no place in the universe that knows not my presence. I participate in all the affairs which those who are without call evil because their nature is not such as they approve. Every age has its own manager, who directs affairs according to my decrees. This office is changeable from generation to generation, that the ruler of this world and his chiefs may discharge the duties of their respective offices every one in his own turn. I allow everyone to follow the dictates of his own nature, but he that opposes me will regret it sorely. No god has a right to interfere in my affairs, and I have made it an imperative rule that everyone shall refrain from worshiping all gods. All the books of those who are without are altered by them; and they have declined from them, although they were written by the prophets and the apostles. That there are interpolations is seen in the fact that each sect endeavors to prove that the others are wrong and to destroy their books. To me truth and falsehood are known. When temptation comes, I give my covenant to him that trusts in me. Moreover, I give counsel to the skilled directors, for I have appointed them for periods that are known to me. I remember necessary affairs and execute them in due time. I teach and guide those who follow my instruction. If anyone obey me and conform to my commandments, he shall have joy, delight, and goodness.

CHAPTER II

I requite the descendants of Adam, and reward them with various rewards that I alone know. Moreover, power and dominion over all that is on earth, both that which is above and that which is beneath, are in my hand. I do not allow friendly association with other people, nor do I deprive them that are my own and that obey me of anything that is good for them. I place my affairs in the hands of those whom I have tried and who are in accord with my desires. I appear in divers manners to those who are faithful and under my command. I give and take away; I enrich and impoverish; I cause both happiness and misery. I do all this in keeping with the characteristics of each epoch. And none has a right to interfere with my management of affairs. Those who oppose me I afflict with disease; but my own shall not die like the sons of Adam that are without. None shall live in this world longer than the time set by me; and if I so desire, I send a person a second or a third time into this world or into some other by the transmigration of souls.

CHAPTER III

I lead to the straight path without a revealed book; I direct aright my beloved and my chosen ones by unseen means. All my teachings are easily applicable to all times and all conditions. I punish in another world all who do contrary to my will. Now the sons of Adam do not know the state of things that is to come. For this reason they fall into many errors. The beasts of the earth, the birds of heaven, and the fish of the sea are all under the control of my hands. All treasures and hidden things are known to me; and as I desire, I take them from one and bestow them upon another. I reveal my wonders to those who seek them, and, in due time my miracles to those who receive them from me. But those who are without are my adversaries, hence they oppose me. Nor do they know that such a course is against their own interests, for might, wealth, and riches are in my hand, and I bestow them upon every worthy descendant of Adam. Thus the government of the worlds, the transition of generations, and the changes of their directors are determined by me from the beginning.

CHAPTER IV

I will not give my rights to other gods. I have allowed the creation of four substances, four times, and four corners; because they are necessary things for creatures. The books of Jews, Christians, and Moslems, as of those who are without, accept in a sense, *i.e.*, so far as they agree with, and conform to, my statutes. Whatsoever is contrary to these they have altered; do not accept it. Three things are against me, and I hate three things. But those who keep my secrets shall receive the fulfillment of my promises. Those who suffer for my sake I will surely reward in one of the worlds. It is my desire that all my followers shall unite in a bond of unity, lest those who are without prevail against them. Now, then, all ye who have followed my commandments and my teachings, reject all the teachings and sayings of such as are without. I have not taught these teachings, nor do they proceed from me. Do not mention my name nor my attributes, lest ye regret it; for ye do not know what those who are without may do.

CHAPTER V

O ye that have believed in me, honor my symbol and my image, for they remind you of me. Observe my laws and statutes. Obey my servants and listen to whatever they may dictate to you of the hidden things. Receive that that is dictated, and do not carry it before those who are without, Jews, Christians, Moslems, and others; for they know not the nature of my teaching. Do not give them your books, lest they alter them without your knowledge. Learn by heart the greater part of them, lest they be altered.

The Poem in Praise of Sheik ‘Adî

My understanding surrounds the truth of things,
And my truth is mixed up in me,
And the truth of my descent is set forth by itself,
And when it was known it was altogether in me.
And all that are in the universe are under me,
And all the habitable parts and deserts,
And everything created is under me,
And I am the ruling power preceding all that exists.
And I am he that spoke a true saying,
And I am the just judge and the ruler of the earth.
And I am he that men worship in my glory,
Coming to me and kissing my feet.
And I am he that spread over the heavens their
    height.
And I am he that cried in the beginning.
And I am he that of myself revealeth all things,
And I am he to whom came the book of good tidings
From my Lord, who burneth the mountains.
And I am he to whom all created men come
In obedience to kiss my feet.
I bring forth fruit from the first juice of early youth
By my presence, and turn toward me my disciples.
And before this light the darkness of the morning
    cleared away.
I guide him that asketh for guidance.
I am he that caused Adam to dwell in Paradise
And Nimrod to inhabit a hot burning fire.

And I am he that guided Ahmed the Just,
And let him into my path and way.
And I am he unto whom all creatures
Come for my good purposes and gifts.
And I am he that visited all the heights,
And goodness and charity proceed from my mercy.
And I am he that made all hearts to fear
My purpose, and they magnify the majesty and power of my awfulness.
And I am he to whom the destroying lion came
Raging, and I shouted against him and he became stone.
And I am he to whom the serpent came,
And by my will I made him dust.
And I am he that struck the rock and made it tremble,
And made to burst from its sides the sweetest of waters.
And I am he that sent down the certain truth;
For me is the book that comforteth the oppressed.
And I am he that judged justly,
And when I judged it was my right
And I am he that made the springs to give water,
Sweeter and pleasanter than all waters.
And I am he that caused it to appear in my mercy,
And by my power I called it the pure.
And I am he to whom the Lord of heaven hath said,
Thou art the just Judge and Ruler of the earth.
And I am he that disclosed some of my wonders,
And some of my virtues are manifested in that which exists.
And I am he that caused the mountains to bow,
To move under me and at my will.
And I am he before whose majesty the wild beasts cried;

They turned to me worshiping, and kissed my feet.
And I am 'Adi ash-Shami, the son of Musafir.
Verily the All-Merciful has assigned unto me names,
The heavenly throne, and the seat, and the (seven) heavens, and the earth.
In the secret of my knowledge there is no God but me.
These things are subservient to my power.
O mine enemies, why do you deny me?
O men, deny me not, but submit.
In the day of judgment you will be happy in meeting me.
Who dies in my love, I will cast him
In the midst of Paradise, by my will and pleasure;
But he that dies unmindful of me
Will be thrown into torture in misery and affliction.
I say I am the only one and the exalted;
I create and make rich those whom I will.
Praise it to myself, for all things are by my will,
And the universe is lighted by some of my gifts.
I am the king that magnifies himself,
And all the riches of creation are at my bidding.
I have made known unto you, O people, some of my ways.
Who desireth me must forsake the world.
And I can also speak the true saying,
And the garden on high is for those who do my pleasure.
I sought the truth and became a confirming truth;
And by the like truth shall they, like myself, possess the highest place.

AL-JILWAH COMMENTARY

THIS is Brother Nero's commentary on the *Al-Jilwah*. These are his personal opinions and should not be taken as doctrine. They are only being included here to give the student insight that they might otherwise overlook. The *Al-Jilwah* is in bold, while the commentary is in plain text.

CHAPTER I

I was, am now, and shall have no end.

"I was" is a very important statement in this line, because it seems to be a response to those who say that Satan is a creation of man. It also seems to be a very declarative statement that says, "I was," meaning before you and everything that exists, "I am," meaning that I still exist, whether you believe in my literal existence or not, and shall have no end. The statement "and shall have no end" seems to be a response to those who suggest that Satan will be destroyed in the end. I hold to the view that even if Satan were to be destroyed in some way, that his will, his desire for self-preservation, and his love for his own existence are so strong, that even if there were the slightest flicker of energy from which he was made, he would be reborn again, much in the same way as the phoenix rises from the ashes. A phoenix is a mythical bird with a tail of beautiful gold and red plumage (or purple and blue, by some sources). It has a 1,000 year life-cycle, and near the end the phoenix builds itself a nest of cinnamon twigs that it then ignites; both nest and bird burn fiercely and are reduced to ashes, from which a new, young phoenix or phoenix egg arises, reborn anew to live again. The new phoenix is destined to live as long as its old self. In some stories, the new phoenix embalms the ashes of its old self in an egg made of myrrh and deposits it in the Egyptian city of Heliopolis ("sun city" in Greek). The bird was also said to regenerate when hurt or wounded by a foe, thus being almost immortal and invincible — it is also said that it can heal a person with a tear from its eyes and make them temporarily immune to death; a symbol of fire and divinity. (Source: Wikipedia)

It is also interesting to note that in the book of Revelation, the Beast that rises from the sea is said to have a similar ability to heal itself. The Beast, it is said, is given its power by the Dragon, who is the Devil, Satan. "And I saw one of his heads as it were wounded to death; and his deadly wound was healed: and all the world wondered after the beast. And they worshipped the dragon which gave power unto the beast: and they worshipped the beast, saying, Who is like unto the beast? who is able to make war with him?" (Revelation 13:3-4)

I exercise dominion over all creatures and over the affairs of all who are under the protection of my image.

The American Heritage® Dictionary of the English Language, Fourth Edition, defines "dominion" this way: "Control or the exercise of control; sovereignty: '*The devil . . . has their souls in his possession, and under his dominion" (Jonathan Edwards).*" I couldn't have said it better myself, so I won't. As far as the reference to "under the protection of my image," I think this statement is pretty self-explanatory, when you consider that most Satanists use the image of Baphomet as part of their religious worship, and within the pentagram. In my mind, it would also be acceptable to use the image of a peacock in addition to the image of the Sabbatic goat.

I am ever present to help all who trust in me and call upon me in time of need.

While this statement may seem pretty selfexplanatory, I feel it is very important that I point out two key phrases in this sentence. First, Satan says, "I am ever present to help all who **trust** in me." The key word here is "trust." Satan will sometimes allow his followers to suffer misfortune if he feels they need to be taught a lesson about trusting him. If you do not trust Satan, he will not help you. You have to absolutely trust that he knows what is best for you and will help shape circumstances to ultimately come out in your favor. If you doubt him, you may end up paying a heavy price, and this price may be necessary if you are a particularly stubborn person. The second important phrase in this sentence is "in time of need." The most important word in this portion of the sentence is "need." Satan will often intervene on our behalf when there is a genuine need for his assistance. It does not mean that he will always intervene when we want him to, but he will intervene when we need him to. Many people make the mistake of thinking just because they want Satan's help, he will give it to them, but Satan is a true and just judge, and he knows the truth of all things, so therefore he intervenes when it is necessary.

There is no place in the universe that knows not my presence.

This statement indicates that Satan is omnipresent.

I participate in all the affairs which those who are without call evil because their nature is not such as they approve.

The majority of religious traditions, but the Abrahamic religious traditions in particular, base their entire philosophy on the idea that everything that is natural to man, whether it is the desire to gain material wealth, the desire for sexual gratification, or the desire to eat to one's heart's content, is evil. The god of the Abrahamic religious traditions has designed his religions to be at odds with the very nature of man's soul, so that he feels like a worthless wretch unworthy to be in his presence. So it is not surprising that they would consider Satan, by whatever name he is called, the Lord of Evil, because he is essentially a nature god that accepts humans for what they are and doesn't make them feel guilty about what is natural to them. The very religious practices and observances of these religions are at odds with nature, and the reasons for this are twofold. First, if the religions make everything that is natural to man a sin, then the adherents to these religions will always feel worthless and be wracked with guilt over their imperfections, which not only gives their god power to maintain his existence, but because they will never be able to fully suppress their natural desires, they will always be in conflict with themselves, and this guilt is what helps their god, churches, synagogues, and mosques maintain power over them. That is why Satan says he participates in all the affairs that those who are without call evil. "Those who are without" is referring to those who are followers of religions that are at odds with the nature of man, and that is why he says their nature is not such as they approve, because the followers of these religions are at odds with their very nature. This is one of the distinguishing characteristics of right-hand path religion, or religions that are devoted to giving up one's individuality and free will. Left-hand path religions on the other hand – religions that our tradition believes were inspired by Satan – champion individuality, encourage free will, and are in harmony with nature.

Every age has its own manager, who directs affairs

according to my decrees. This office is changeable from generation to generation, that the ruler of this world and his chiefs may discharge the duties of their respective offices every one in his own turn.

This statement has at least a twofold meaning. First, this statement seems to suggest that Satan has appointed certain deities to rule over certain epochs, and they are changeable from time to time, according to Satan's will and desire. Secondly, it seems to suggest that Satan has control over the leaders of kingdoms and governments of earth, and decides how long they shall stay in power, as well as who shall succeed them. It is also safe to assume that if Satan determines who will rule a certain epoch in a spiritual sense, and who the rulers will be in an earthly sense, that he appoints the leaders of his religious orders for a time that is known only to him. Likewise, he determines who their successors will be, just as he does in every other sense.

I allow everyone to follow the dictates of his own nature, but he that opposes me will regret it sorely.

Satan allows everybody to be themselves and do what they want to do, as long as who they want to be and what they want to do does not conflict with his goals and desires, either for them or for his cause.

No god has a right to interfere in my affairs, and I have made it an imperative rule that everyone shall refrain from worshiping all gods.

At first glance, this passage may give many Satanists pause, because it seems to be at odds with worshiping the demons in addition to Satan, but I believe this passage is referring to any god or entity that is not loyal to Satan and under his authority. So if you worship a demon who is under his authority and submits to his will, you are not contradicting this passage.

All the books of those who are without are altered by them; and they have declined from them, although they were written by the prophets and the apostles.

The phrase "all the books of those who are without are altered by them" is a clear reference to the fact that the texts of the Abrahamic religions in particular are considered infallible, but it is a well-known fact that almost any religious text that has been around for any length of time is often altered by its adherents. One group will alter the text by taking something out, and another group will alter the text by putting something in, and over time, the original language and meaning of the text will either be completely lost or altered so dramatically that it's hard to clearly discern the text's true meaning. An excellent example of how texts can be manipulated to present someone in a negative light can be seen in the Christian Bible. The Christian Bible admits that it is not a full account of all the events that happened. If the Bible admits that it does not give a full account of what happened, what else has been left out that the authors of the Bible would not admit? For example, if you believe as the Protestants do that the Bible was inspired by the Christian god, and its very compilation was guided by his hand, then it is obvious that the Bible is not going to give an accurate account of what actually happened during the creation process, and they would leave anything out of the Bible that would present Satan in a positive light, even if it was at odds with the events that actually occurred during the creation. Satan is giving a clear warning to those who believe that the holy texts of the Abrahamic religions are infallible that they have been altered by their adherents, and have not given an accurate account of the facts surrounding the creation of the universe, earth, or man. Many people, especially those who are practitioners of a faith, tend to believe that their holy texts are infallible. Satan makes it clear that they are not.

That there are interpolations is seen in the fact that each sect endeavors to prove that the others are wrong and to destroy their books. To me truth and falsehood are known. When temptation comes, I give my covenant to him that trusts in me.

In this passage, Satan re-emphasizes again the importance of his children having trust in him. If you don't trust in him, and you doubt him, he will be less likely to help you. Satanists must always bear in mind, no matter how bleak a situation may be, no matter how insurmountable the odds may seem, more often than not, if you just trust in Satan, it will all fall into place the way it's meant to be in the end.

Moreover, I give counsel to the skilled directors, for I have appointed them for periods that are known to me. I remember necessary affairs and execute them in due time. I teach and guide those who follow my instruction. If anyone obey me and conform to my commandments, he shall have joy, delight, and goodness.

I believe these passages are directed towards the priesthood of the groups which are loyal to him, stressing to them that he does give guidance to those who are loyal and trying their best to do his will. It also indicates that he has already predestined how long they will serve in the positions that have been granted to them. He stresses that he does things according to his time line, not ours. He also points out to his priesthood and his followers that he deals with things when he feels they are important, not when we may feel they are important.

I requite the descendents of Adam, and reward them with various rewards that I alone know. Moreover, power and dominion over all that is on earth, both that which is above and that which is beneath, are in my hand.

Here, Satan reaffirms the point that he is the one who holds the destiny of man and earth in his hands, not the Judeo-Christian god.

I do not allow friendly association with other people, nor do I deprive them that are my own and that obey me of anything that is good for them.

This passage is the basis of our belief that Satanists should not marry, have children, or have friends outside of their religion. They should keep to themselves and not associate with people who are not Satanists. While some Satanists may see this as an extreme point of view, Satan also seems to address this by saying "nor do I deprive them that are my own and that obey me of anything that is good for them." You can find everything that you need within the confines of the Satanic community, whether it be friendship, love, relationships, etc. While Satanists should look to each other for their basic needs, it is okay to use those who are without to achieve your goals, but you should always remember that they are without – they are not your brothers, they are not your sisters, they are not your family. They are dirt. They are cattle. They are slaves. They are unmindful of Satan, so Satan's children should be unmindful of them. They should be associated with only if it helps Satan's cause or helps you achieve your personal desires.

I place my affairs in the hands of those whom I have tried and who are in accord with my desires.

This passage makes it clear that Satan does test his followers and his priesthood, and expects them to earn their place within his kingdom.

I appear in divers manners to those who are faithful and under my command.

Melek Ta'us, Satan, Ahriman, Set, etc. are all manifestations of the Lord of Darkness.

I give and take away; I enrich and impoverish; I cause both happiness and misery. I do all this in keeping with the characteristics of each epoch. And none has a right to interfere with my management of affairs. Those who oppose me I afflict with disease; but my own shall not die like the sons of Adam that are without. None shall live in this world longer than the time set by me; and if I so desire, I send a person a second or a third time into this world or into some other by the transmigration of souls.

This passage shows that Satan is the one who has control over how long any of his children shall live, and it also makes clear that he has in the past, and does still now, grant the privilege of reincarnation to those he deems worthy of reincarnation to do his will, as many times as he sees fit.

CHAPTER III

I lead to the straight path without a revealed book; I direct aright my beloved and my chosen ones by unseen means.

Many people often ask, "Does traditional Satanism have a Bible?" and they are surprised to find out that it does not. There are many texts that we believe are inspired, but there is no "Bible," and Satan seems to address this directly in this passage. The *Al-Jilwah* is the only text that comes even remotely close to being universally accepted by most traditional Satanists, but even the *Al-Jilwah* is not accepted as a sacred text by all Satanists. The portion of this passage that refers to "unseen means," in my mind, is clearly referring to those individual spiritual experiences that every real Satanist has. It is that internal guidance or internal voice that directs them where they should be going. H.O.M.E. used to refer to this as the *genius*, which is defined as "the guardian spirit of a man or place," (Cassell's *Latin Dictionary*), or internal tutor. This is that portion of Satan's essence that dwells within the heart of every Satanist, that gives them guidance when they need it. Interestingly enough, this spiritual essence or internal voice was symbolized in medieval artwork as a raven, which sat on the magician's shoulder and whispered in his ear, giving him words of guidance from Satan. This was the opposing symbol to the image of the dove, which symbolized the holy spirit.

All my teachings are easily applicable to all times and all conditions.

Satan makes it clear that the essence of his teachings and philosophy don't change according to the whims of man. They are timeless.

I punish in another world all who do contrary to my will. Now the sons of Adam do not know the state of things that is to come. For this reason they fall into many errors.

In my mind, this passage is clearly referring to those who deem themselves prophets, especially those who adhere to the Abrahamic religious traditions, because the descendents of Adam clearly refers to those who consider themselves to be descendents of Adam, which are the Christians, Muslims, and Jews.

The beasts of the earth, the birds of heaven, and the fish of the sea are all under the control of my hands. All treasures and hidden things are known to me; and as I desire, I take them from one and bestow them upon another.

This passage clearly indicates that Satan exercises dominion over the affairs of man and the things of earth, and has the power to bestow upon people material and spiritual wealth as he sees fit.

I reveal my wonders to those who seek them, and, in due time my miracles to those who receive them from me.

This passage seems to indicate that if a follower seeks him with sincere, heartfelt desire, they will eventually receive the reward of his gifts and miracles.

But those who are without are my adversaries, hence they oppose me. Nor do they know that such a course is against their own interests, for might, wealth, and riches are in my hand, and I bestow them upon every worthy descendant of Adam. Thus the government of the worlds, the transition of generations, and the changes of their directors are determined by me from the beginning.

This passage clearly indicates that Satan is omniscient and has the ability to control the appointment of kings and the establishment of governments. He also has the ability to control the more mundane affairs of man, such as marriage, procreation, etc. However, it is unclear to what degree he avails himself of this power, as it is him who gave us the gift of free will in the first place.

CHAPTER IV

I will not give my rights to other gods.

Again, Satan emphasizes that he will not give his rights and authority to any other god. I believe that means any god that is not loyal to him – gods of right-hand path religions in particular. This does not, in my opinion, refer to demons because those are gods that are under his command and submit to his will. This passage is talking about gods that are not loyal to him.

I have allowed the creation of four substances, four times, and four comers; because they are necessary things for creatures. The books of Jews, Christians, and Moslems, as of those who are without, accept in a sense, so far as they agree with, and conform to, my statutes. Whatsoever is contrary to these they have altered; do not accept it.

This passage shows that there are elements of truth even in the holy texts of those who are without. For example, even the Bible says that Satan is the ruler of this earth and has the kingdoms of the world in his hands. "And the devil, taking him up into an high mountain, showed unto him all the kingdoms of the world in a moment of time. And the devil said unto him, All this power will I give thee, and the glory of them: for that is delivered unto me; and to whomsoever I will I give it. If thou therefore wilt worship me, all shall be thine." (Luke 4:5-8) As Satan instructs, omit everything that isn't true from the texts of those who are without, and keep only that which is true and that agrees with what he says, and you have his word. In the case of the Bible, this leaves us with only a few statements. The one I have included in the commentary is one of the few.

Three things are against me, and I hate three things.

Generally, this statement is accepted among Satanists to mean one of two things: it either refers to the religions of Christianity, Judaism, and Islam, or is a reference to the Father, the Son, and the Holy Ghost. I am sure that there are other groups out there who have other ideas or believe it refers to something else entirely, but I believe it refers to the traditions of the Abrahamic faiths in particular.

But those who keep my secrets shall receive the fulfillment of my promises.

This statement seems to indicate that if you keep your oaths of secrecy to Satan, and you keep quiet about your communications with him and his demons, he will reward you. It is generally held by most occultists that your communication with the demonic spirits is to be kept secret and not shared even with your fellow Satanists. If it is shared, it is only amongst those who you most trust and truly consider your brothers and sisters in Satanism, i.e. the members of your coven.

Those who suffer for my sake I will surely reward in one of the worlds.

Many Satanists tend to complain about the injustices that they suffer as a result of their loyalty to Satan. It should come as no surprise to any Satanist that we are persecuted for our beliefs and our loyalty to Satan. When you worship someone who is the enemy of this Judeo-

Christian-based society we live in, one cannot expect not to be persecuted for worshiping him. If we carry ourselves with pride, dignity, and honor and remember that we are first and foremost to be loyal to Satan and his kingdom before everything else, then Satan says that he will reward us for our loyalty and for any persecution which we have suffered in his name. Having our civil rights violated and being ridiculed for worshiping Satan is just part of the job; it's what we signed up for when we became Satanists, and if you're not willing to accept that, then maybe you really aren't a Satanist. When you start to feel bad about the way you are being treated, you should try to think about it from Satan's point of view. He is hated by the majority of mankind simply for being who he is. So if he can maintain his pride and his dignity through all that he suffered, then so can we.

It is my desire that all my followers shall unite in a bond of unity, lest those who are without prevail against them.

For further comment, please refer to "Chapter 3: Satanic Unity and the Antichrist" in this volume for my comment on this passage.

Now, then, all ye who have followed my commandments and my teachings, reject all the teachings and sayings of such as are without. I have not taught these teachings, nor do they proceed from me.

While this is clearly talking about those who are without, such as Christians, Muslims, Jews, etc., it can also be applied to those who pretend to have communication with Satan. In my years of experience as a Satanist, I have found that Satan and demons are amazingly consistent in what they teach their followers, and while they may present the teachings in different ways to suit the different people they deal with, the essence of the teachings never changes. For example, it is almost universally accepted without question by Satanists that Satan allows his children to follow their own nature, so long as they do not oppose him. "I allow everyone to follow the dictates of his own nature, but he that opposes me will regret it sorely." If I were reading a text, and the text claimed to be the direct word of Satan, and it had statements that were contrary to the teachings of Satan, especially those that Satan and demons have always been consistent on, I would disregard the text as a fake. Satan's core teachings do not change, and that is what I believe Satan is referring to here when he says "Reject all the teachings and sayings of such as are without."

Do not mention my name nor my attributes, lest ye regret it; for ye do not know what those who are without may do.

Anton LaVey insisted that this command no longer applied to Satanists in our day and age. I believe there is evidence to suggest otherwise. If we look at what happens to the majority of Satanists when they proudly proclaim they are Satanists, whether it is in the courtroom or on the job, we can see that people are still persecuted and abused for believing in Satan. If one chooses to mention his name and attributes in direct defiance of Satan's instruction, the person who mentions his name and attributes must take responsibility for their choices, and they cannot blame Satan if they are abused as a result, because he has warned them about what may happen if they do so.

CHAPTER V

O ye that have believed in me, honor my symbol and my image, for they remind you of me.

I take this statement to be a reference to the symbol of the pentagram and the image of the Baphomet or the Sabbatic goat.

Observe my laws and statutes. Obey my servants and listen to whatever they may dictate to you of the hidden things.

This passage is referring not only to his earthly priesthood, but to those messages which a Satanist receives from the demonic spirits. As a matter of fact, Demons do communicate with true followers of Satan fairly regularly. It is not uncommon for people to receive inspired dreams and messages from the spirit world, and Satan instructs us to obey his messengers, and listen to whatever they may tell us about the hidden things, which is clearly a reference to the spirit world and the workings of his kingdom.

Receive that that is dictated, and do not carry it before those who are without, Jews, Christians, Moslems, and others; for they know not the nature of my teaching.

This is clearly an indication that when you receive a message from the spirit world, you are not to share it with individuals who are without. The reason you are not supposed to share them with those who are without is because they do not understand the nature of Satan or the nature of his teachings.

Do not give them your books, lest they alter them without your knowledge. Learn by heart the greater part of them, lest they be altered.

Satan gave the Yezidis instructions not to reveal their books to anyone. They clearly did not listen. We can all see what happened to the *Al-Jilwah* as a result. It has been changed and edited in a myriad of different ways which the Yezidis could not have foreseen, whether it is people adding chapters or omitting chapters, or adding things to it so that the *Al-Jilwah* will say what they want it to say to support their philosophy. If the Yezidis had listened to Satan, this would not have happened. What does this teach us? That when you disobey Satan, everything that he says will happen comes to pass, proving that he is not only a god of his word, but that he is omniscient. It also proves that he can shape circumstances in such a way to use even our mistakes to his benefit, as we can see from the Yezidi example. That is why I encourage everyone to learn the *Al-Jilwah* by heart as Satan commanded, so that we will not be misled by people who seek to alter the *Al-Jilwah* to further their own ends.

CONTACT BROTHER NERO

www.RJWomack.com

https://www.facebook.com/rjwomack15/

https://twitter.com/rjwo15

If you enjoyed this book, please help me
out by leaving me a review at:

https://www.amazon.com/Brother-Nero/e/B00O0M08X8

Thanks,
Nero

37345176R00094

Printed in Great Britain
by Amazon